DATE DUE

Mindfulness and Meditation

**Recent Titles in
Q&A Health Guides**

Self-Injury: Your Questions Answered
Romeo Vitelli

Living Green: Your Questions Answered
Amy Hackney Blackwell

Sexually Transmitted Diseases: Your Questions Answered
Paul Quinn

MINDFULNESS AND MEDITATION

Your Questions Answered

Blaise Aguirre

Q&A Health Guides

An Imprint of ABC-CLIO, LLC
Santa Barbara, California • Denver, Colorado

Library of Congress Cataloging-in-Publication Data

Names: Aguirre, Blaise A., author.
Title: Mindfulness and meditation : your questions answered / Blaise Aguirre.
Description: Santa Barbara, California : Greenwood, [2018] | Series: Q&A
    health guides | Includes bibliographical references and index.
Identifiers: LCCN 2017056251 (print) | LCCN 2017059584 (ebook) |
    ISBN 9781440852978 (ebook) | ISBN 9781440852961 (alk. paper)
Subjects: LCSH: Mindfulness (Psychology) | Meditation.
Classification: LCC BF637.M4 (ebook) | LCC BF637.M4 A385 2018 (print) |
    DDC 158.1/2—dc23
LC record available at https://lccn.loc.gov/2017056251

ISBN: 978-1-4408-5296-1 (print)
       978-1-4408-5297-8 (ebook)

22 21 20 19 18   1 2 3 4 5

This book is also available as an eBook.

Greenwood
An Imprint of ABC-CLIO, LLC

ABC-CLIO, LLC
130 Cremona Drive, P.O. Box 1911
Santa Barbara, California 93116–1911
www.abc-clio.com

This book is printed on acid-free paper (∞)

Manufactured in the United States of America

To my family, who mindfully accept that I am writing yet another book, even after I have said "last one," to all my patients who have shown me and continue to show me the healing power of mindfulness, and to my editor Maxine Taylor who skillfully moved me from not writing another book to getting this one done!

Contents

Series Foreword   ix

Preface   xi

Acknowledgments   xiii

Guide to Health Literacy   xv

Common Misconceptions about Mindfulness and Meditation   xxiii

Questions and Answers   **1**

What Mindfulness Is and What It Is Not   3

    1. What is mindfulness?   3
    2. Why is mindfulness relevant?   7
    3. What is meditation?   9
    4. What are reasons to practice?   11
    5. Is mindfulness the same as yoga or relaxation? 14
    6. What is enlightenment?   16
    7. Are there different types of meditation?   18
    8. When is focused attention *not* mindfulness?   20
    9. Isn't mindfulness just a fad that will come and go? 21

How to Practice Mindfulness   25

    10. Can anyone practice?   25
    11. How do you practice mindfulness?   28
    12. What is a meditation retreat?   30

13. What makes for a good mindfulness teacher? 33
14. Do I need to practice every day, and if so, how long before I see a difference? 36
15. Can I do other things, like listening to music, while I meditate? 38
16. Isn't it better if I use mindfulness time for planning my day and doing things? 40
17. How do I deal with distractions? 43
18. Is it okay if I move around while I meditate? 45
19. What if I am the only one of my friends practicing? 47
20. How do drugs and alcohol impact mindfulness? 49

The Historical Origins of Mindfulness 53

21. Is mindfulness a religion? 53
22. Is mindfulness practice compatible with different religions? 55
23. When did mindfulness come to the United States? 60
24. Are there famous people who practice mindfulness? 63

Research and Applications 67

25. How is research on mindfulness conducted? 67
26. What does research show about mindfulness and interpersonal relationships? 70
27. What does research show about mindfulness and specific mental disorders? 72
28. Is there any research on the physical health benefits of mindfulness? 76
29. Can mindfulness help in sports? 79
30. Can mindfulness help in academics? 83
31. Can mindfulness help in the business world? 86
32. What does research say about mindful eating? 87

Mindfulness and the Modern World 91

33. How does being continually connected to multiple electronic devices impact mindfulness? 91
34. What is the impact of social media on mindfulness? 94
35. Can apps help someone be mindful? 96

Case Studies 99

Glossary 111

Directory of Resources 113

Index 123

Series Foreword

All of us have questions about our health. Is this normal? Should I be doing something differently? Who should I talk to about my concerns? And our modern world is full of answers. Thanks to the Internet, there's a wealth of information at our fingertips, from forums where people can share their personal experiences to Wikipedia articles to the full text of medical studies. But finding the right information can be an intimidating and difficult task—some sources are written at too high a level, others have been oversimplified, while still others are heavily biased or simply inaccurate.

Q&A Health Guides address the needs of readers who want accurate, concise answers to their health questions, authored by reputable and objective experts, and written in clear and easy-to-understand language. This series focuses on the topics that matter most to young adult readers, including various aspects of physical and emotional well-being, as well as other components of a healthy lifestyle. These guides will also serve as a valuable tool for parents, school counselors, and others who may need to answer teens' health questions.

All books in the series follow the same format to make finding information quick and easy. Each volume begins with an essay on health literacy and why it is so important when it comes to gathering and evaluating health information. Next, the top five myths and misconceptions that surround the topic are dispelled. The heart of each guide is a collection of questions and answers, organized thematically. A selection of five case studies provides real-world examples to illuminate key concepts. Rounding out each volume are a glossary, directory of resources, and index.

It is our hope that the books in this series will not only provide valuable information but also help guide readers toward a lifetime of healthy decision making.

Preface

I arrived at Harvard's McLean Hospital in May 2000 to start work on the adolescent unit. At that time I knew nothing about a new treatment known as dialectical behavior therapy (DBT), which had previously been used to treat suicidal women. McLean was pioneering DBT in adolescents.

Core to DBT is the practice of mindfulness, and although the concept is easy to articulate in theory, the practice and experience is more nuanced. We opened a dedicated DBT unit for adolescents in 2007 and with that I decided that I needed a much deeper understanding of mindfulness.

With that I headed out to Tucson and the Redemptorist Renewal Center in the Sonoran desert. It is a perfect site for mindfulness practice: located in the foothills of the Tucson Mountains on the edge of the Saguaro National Park.

For the next five days I sat in silence together with my fellow retreatants. The experience changed my life. It taught me how to accept things as they are, to become far less judgmental, to tolerate intense emotions, and to recognize that automatic nature of many of my thoughts and behaviors. I noticed that I was far less anxious than I had ever been and, with that, just how powerful mindfulness could be as a tool for healing mental suffering.

This book is a testament to the broad utility of mindfulness and an exploration of the practice beyond its use in mental and physical well-being.

Acknowledgments

Over the years I have had the opportunity to practice mindfulness meditation in various contexts and with many different people.

I want to recognize the people who have traveled with me on my journey. First, I have deep appreciation for Dr. Marsha Linehan, the developer of DBT, who emphasized the importance of mindfulness as central to mental health and mental healing.

Then to my colleagues at 3East and in particular Janna Hobbs, Michael Hollander, Judy Mintz, and Gillian Galen, who have kept mindfulness central to the work we do every day.

To the Reverend Pat Hawk (may he RIP), leader of the silent retreats in Tucson and the wisest person I ever knew, I thank you. To Zen teacher and fellow DBT trainer Randy Wolpert, gratitude for showing that mindfulness is not all that serious.

I appreciate the teachings of Thich Nhat Hanh, Tara Brach, and Sharon Salzberg, whose writings have deepened my practice; then Larry Kasanoff, for bringing mindfulness to the lay community in our movie *Mindfulness: Be Happy Now*; to Oprah and Becky Sykes, who get the importance of mindfulness practice in education and wellness.

Finally to my family, who never complain when I leave for a silent retreat and then give me plenty of opportunities to show how much work I have left to do.

Guide to Health Literacy

On her 13th birthday, Samantha was diagnosed with type 2 diabetes. She consulted her mom and her aunt, both of whom also have type 2 diabetes, and decided to go with their strategy of managing diabetes by taking insulin. As a result of participating in an after-school program at her middle school that focused on health literacy, she learned that she can help manage the level of glucose in her bloodstream by counting her carbohydrate intake, following a diabetic diet, and exercising regularly. But, what exactly should she do? How does she keep track of her carbohydrate intake? What is a diabetic diet? How long should she exercise and what type of exercise should she do? Samantha is a visual learner, so she turned to her favorite source of media, YouTube, to answer these questions. She found videos from individuals around the world sharing their experiences and tips, doctors (or at least people who have "Dr." in their YouTube channel names), and government agencies such as the National Institutes of Health, and even video clips from cat lovers who have cats with diabetes. With guidance from the librarian and the health and science teachers at her school, she assessed the credibility of the information in these videos and even compared their suggestions to some of the print resources that she was able to find at her school library. Now, she knows exactly how to count her carbohydrate level, how to prepare and follow a diabetic diet, and how much (and what) exercise is needed daily. She intends to share her findings with her mom and her aunt, and now she wants to create a chart that summarizes what she has learned that she can share with her doctor.

Samantha's experience is not unique. She represents a shift in our society; an individual no longer views himself or herself as a passive recipient of medical care but as an active mediator of his or her own health. However, in this era when any individual can post his or her opinions and experiences with a particular health condition online with just a few clicks or publish a memoir, it is vital that people know how to assess the credibility of health information. Gone are the days when "publishing" health information required intense vetting. The health information landscape is highly saturated, and people have innumerable sources where they can find information about practically any health topic. The sources (whether print, online, or a person) that an individual consults for health information are crucial because the accuracy and trustworthiness of the information can potentially affect his or her overall health. The ability to find, select, assess, and use health information constitutes a type of literacy—health literacy—that everyone must possess.

THE DEFINITION AND PHASES OF HEALTH LITERACY

One of the most popular definitions for health literacy comes from Ratzan and Parker (2000), who describe health literacy as "the degree to which individuals have the capacity to obtain, process, and understand basic health information and services needed to make appropriate health decisions." Recent research has extrapolated health literacy into health literacy bits, further shedding light on the multiple phases and literacy practices that are embedded within the multifaceted concept of health literacy. Although this research has focused primarily on online health information seeking, these health literacy bits are needed to successfully navigate both print and online sources. There are six phases of health information seeking: (1) Information Need Identification and Question Formulation, (2) Information Search, (3) Information Comprehension, (4) Information Assessment, (5) Information Management, and (6) Information Use.

The first phase is the *information need identification and question formulation* phase. In this phase, one needs to be able to develop and refine a range of questions to frame one's search and understand relevant health terms. In the second phase, *information search,* one has to possess appropriate searching skills, such as using proper keywords and correct spelling in search terms, especially when using search engines and databases. It is also crucial to understand how search engines work (i.e., how search results are derived, what the order of the search results means, how to use the snippets that are provided in the search results list to select websites, and how to determine which listings are ads on a search engine results page). One also has to limit reliance on surface characteristics, such as the design of a website or a book (a website or book that appears to have a lot of information or looks aesthetically pleasant does not necessarily mean it has good information) and language used (a website or book that utilizes jargon, the keywords that one used to conduct the search, or the word "information" does not necessarily indicate it will have good information). The next phase is *information comprehension*, whereby one needs to have the ability to read, comprehend, and recall the information (including textual, numerical, and visual content) one has located from the books and/or online resources.

To assess the credibility of health information (*information assessment* phase), one needs to be able to evaluate information for accuracy, evaluate how current the information is (e.g., when a website was last updated or when a book was published), and evaluate the creators of the source—for example, examine site sponsors or type of sites (.com, .gov, .edu, or .org) or the author of a book (practicing doctor, a celebrity doctor, a patient of a specific disease, etc.)—to determine the believability of the person/organization providing the information. Such credibility perceptions tend to become generalized, so they must be frequently reexamined (e.g., the belief that a specific news agency always has credible health information needs continuous vetting). One also needs to evaluate the credibility of the medium (e.g., television, Internet, radio, social media, and book) and evaluate—not just accept without questioning—others' claims regarding the validity of a site, book, or other specific source of information. At this stage, one has to "make sense of information gathered from diverse sources by identifying misconceptions, main and supporting ideas, conflicting information, point of view, and biases" (American Association of School Librarians [AASL], 2009, p. 13) and conclude which information or sources are valid and accurate by using conscious strategies rather than simply using intuitive judgments or "rules of thumb." This phase is the most challenging segment of health information seeking and serves as a determinant of success (or lack thereof) in the information-seeking process. The following section on Sources of Health Information further explains this phase.

The fifth phase is *information management*, whereby one has to organize information that has been gathered in some manner to ensure easy retrieval and use in the future. The last phase is *information use*, in which one will synthesize information found across various resources, draw conclusions, and locate the answer to one's original question and/or the content that fulfills the information need. This phase also often involves implementation, such as using the information to solve a health problem; make health-related decisions; identify and engage in behaviors that will help a person to avoid health risks; share the health information found with family members and friends who may benefit from it; and advocate more broadly for personal, family, or community health.

THE IMPORTANCE OF HEALTH LITERACY

The conception of health has moved from a passive view (someone is either well or ill) to one that is more active and process based (someone is working toward preventing or managing disease). Hence, the dominant focus has shifted from doctors and treatments to patients and prevention, resulting in the need to strengthen our ability and confidence (as patients and consumers of health care) to look for, assess, understand, manage, share, adapt, and use health-related information. An individual's health literacy level has been found to predict his or her health status better than age, race, educational attainment, employment status, and income level (National Network of Libraries of Medicine, 2013). Greater health literacy also enables individuals to better communicate with health-care providers such as doctors, nutritionists, and therapists, as they can pose more relevant, informed, and useful questions to health-care providers. Another added advantage of greater health literacy is better information-seeking skills, not only for health but also in other domains, such as completing assignments for school.

SOURCES OF HEALTH INFORMATION: THE GOOD, THE BAD, AND THE IN-BETWEEN

For generations, doctors, nurses, nutritionists, health coaches, and other health professionals have been the trusted sources of health information. Additionally, researchers have found that young adults, when they have health-related questions, typically turn to a family member who has had firsthand experience with a health condition because of their family member's close proximity and because of their past experience with, and trust in, this individual. Expertise should be a core consideration when consulting a person, website, or book for health information. The credentials and background of the person or author and conflicting interests of the author (and his or her organization) must be checked and validated to ensure the likely credibility of the health information they are conveying. While books often have implied credibility because of the peer-review process involved, self-publishing has challenged this credibility, so qualifications of book authors should also be verified. When it comes to health information, currency of the source must also be examined. When examining health information/studies presented, pay attention to the exhaustiveness of research methods utilized to offer recommendations or conclusions. Small and nondiverse sample size is often—but not always—an indication of reduced credibility. Studies that confuse correlation with causation is another potential issue to watch for. Information seekers must also pay attention to the sponsors of the research studies. For example, if a study is sponsored by manufacturers of drug Y and the study recommends that drug Y is the best treatment to manage or cure a disease, this may indicate a lack of objectivity on the part of the researchers.

The Internet is rapidly becoming one of the main sources of health information. Online forums, news agencies, personal blogs, social media sites, pharmacy sites, and celebrity "doctors" are all offering medical and health information targeted at various types of people in regard to all types of diseases and symptoms. There are professional journalists, citizen journalists, hoaxers, and people paid to write fake health news on various sites that may appear to have a legitimate domain name and may even have authors who claim to have professional credentials, such as an MD. All these sites *may* offer useful information or information that appears to be useful and relevant; however, much of the information may be debatable and may fall into gray areas that require readers to discern credibility, reliability, and biases.

While broad recognition and acceptance of certain media, institutions, and people often serve as the most popular determining factors to assess credibility of health information among young people, keep in mind that there are legitimate Internet sites, databases, and books that publish health information and serve as sources of health information for doctors, other health sites, and members of the public. For example, MedlinePlus (https://medlineplus.gov) has trusted sources on over 975 diseases and conditions and presents the information in easy-to-understand language.

The chart here presents factors to consider when assessing credibility of health information. However, keep in mind that these factors function only as a guide and require continuous updating to keep abreast with the changes in the landscape of health information, information sources, and technologies.

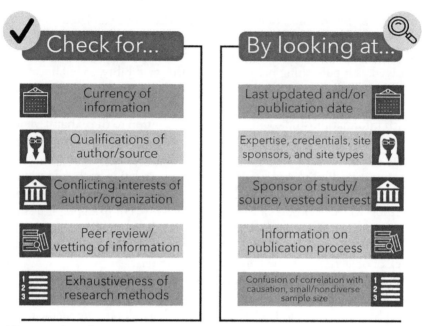

All images from flaticon.com

The chart can serve as a guide; however, approaching a librarian about how one can go about assessing the credibility of both print and online health information is far more effective than using generic checklist-type tools. While librarians are not health experts, they can apply and teach patrons strategies to determine the credibility of health information.

With the prevalence of fake sites and fake resources that appear to be legitimate, it is important to use the following health information assessment tips to verify health information that one has obtained (St. Jean et al., 2015, p. 151):

- *Don't assume you are right:* Even when you feel very sure about an answer, keep in mind that the answer may not be correct, and it is important to conduct (further) searches to validate the information.
- *Don't assume you are wrong:* You may actually have correct information, even if the information you encounter does not match—that is, you may be right and the resources that you have found may contain false information.
- *Take an open approach:* Maintain a critical stance by not including your preexisting beliefs as keywords (or letting them influence your choice of keywords) in a search, as this may influence what it is possible to find out.

- *Verify, verify, and verify:* Information found, especially on the Internet, needs to be validated, no matter how the information appears on the site (i.e., regardless of the appearance of the site or the quantity of information that is included).

Health literacy comes with experience navigating health information. Professional sources of health information, such as doctors, health-care providers, and health databases, are still the best, but one also has the power to search for health information and then verify it by consulting with these trusted sources and by using the health information assessment tips and guide shared previously.

Mega Subramaniam, PhD
Associate Professor, College of Information Studies,
University of Maryland

REFERENCES AND FURTHER READING

American Association of School Librarians (AASL). (2009). *Standards for the 21st-century learner in action.* Chicago, IL: American Association of School Librarians.

Hilligoss, B., & Rieh, S.-Y. (2008). Developing a unifying framework of credibility assessment: Construct, heuristics, and interaction in context. *Information Processing & Management, 44*(4), 1467–1484.

Kuhlthau, C. C. (1988). Developing a model of the library search process: Cognitive and affective aspects. *Reference Quarterly, 28*(2), 232–242.

National Network of Libraries of Medicine (NNLM). (2013). Health literacy. Bethesda, MD: National Network of Libraries of Medicine. Retrieved from nnlm.gov/outreach/consumer/hlthlit.html

Ratzan, S. C., & Parker, R. M. (2000). Introduction. In C. R. Selden, M. Zorn, S. C. Ratzan, & R. M. Parker (Eds.), *National Library of Medicine current bibliographies in medicine: Health literacy.* NLM Publication No. CBM 2000-1. Bethesda, MD: National Institutes of Health, U.S. Department of Health and Human Services.

St. Jean, B., Subramaniam, M., Taylor, N. G., Follman, R., Kodama, C., & Casciotti, D. (2015). The influence of positive hypothesis testing on youths' online health-related information seeking. *New Library World, 116*(3/4), 136–154.

St. Jean, B., Taylor, N. G., Kodama, C., & Subramaniam, M. (February 2017). Assessing the health information source perceptions of tweens using card-sorting exercises. *Journal of Information Science.* Retrieved from http://journals.sagepub.com/doi/abs/10.1177/0165551516687728

Subramaniam, M., St. Jean, B., Taylor, N.G., Kodama, C., Follman, R., & Casciotti, D. (2015). Bit by bit: Using design-based research to improve the health literacy of adolescents. *JMIR Research Protocols, 4*(2), paper e62. Retrieved from http://www.ncbi.nlm.nih.gov/pmc/articles/PMC4464334/

Valenza, J. (2016, November 26). Truth, truthiness, and triangulation: A news literacy toolkit for a "post-truth" world [Web log]. Retrieved from http://blogs.slj.com/neverendingsearch/2016/11/26/truth-truthiness-triangulation-and-the-librarian-way-a-news-literacy-toolkit-for-a-post-truth-world/

❖

Common Misconceptions about Mindfulness and Meditation

1. MINDFULNESS IS FOR TAKING A TIME-OUT FROM LIFE AND RELAXING

This myth likely developed because of the image of people sitting around at retreats with their eyes closed during meditation. Whereas it is true that at first mindfulness can give people a sense of relief from an anxious and overactive mind, mindfulness is not just that. The irony is that fully practicing mindfulness does typically lead to a quieter and less-stressful experience of life, whereas forcibly trying to quiet things down (e.g., by planning an elaborate beach vacation with family or friends) can often make things more stressful. For more information on the differences between mindfulness and relaxing, please see Question 5.

2. YOU NEED TO CARVE OUT PLENTY OF TIME AND SPACE TO DO MINDFULNESS

Mindfulness can be practiced in infinite ways, and what your day looks like determines what works for you. It can be helpful to set aside 20 minutes each day to practice, but it is not necessary. You don't need to fight to carve out the time to do it. Simply be mindful of whatever it is you are doing in the moment, whether showering, having a cup of tea, or walking to school; that is the time and space to practice. For more information, see Questions 14 and 15.

3. YOU NEED TO BE MINDFUL ALL THE TIME

If we were present in each and every moment, we would be overstimulated and overwhelmed because each moment has so much detail. Much of what we do is a reflection of habit and needs to be that way, otherwise we would be stuck in examining each part of each moment. Imagine paying attention to each and every aspect of driving. We wouldn't be able to drive. Our attention has to be on the road and not on the technique of driving. The How to Practice Mindfulness section offers more information about finding appropriate times and situations to practice mindfulness.

4. MINDFULNESS IS USEFUL ONLY FOR REDUCING STRESS

There is a therapy known as mindfulness-based stress reduction (MBSR), and mindfulness has been shown in many research studies to help reduce stress. The many benefits of mindfulness, however, go way beyond stress reduction. In the Research and Applications section, the many benefits of the practice will be reviewed. These will include its utility in areas such as sports, relationships, physical and mental health, and the business world.

5. YOU HAVE TO BE RELIGIOUS TO BE MINDFUL

Although many religions have mindfulness and meditation practices, it is not necessary to be religious to achieve a mindful state. The skill of mindfulness has been broken down by contemporary practitioners so that a person can use the ability outside of a spiritual context, and the value of mindfulness is as beneficial to the devoutly religious person as it is to the nonreligious person. For more information on the intersection of mindfulness and religion, see Questions 21 and 22.

QUESTIONS AND ANSWERS

What Mindfulness Is and What It Is Not

1. What is mindfulness?

Imagine that you go into your local coffee shop each morning and order a decaf latte made with skimmed milk. You are well known to the baristas, and they greet you as you walk in and start making your latte even before you have placed your order. You like that they know you by name and that they take such good care of you. It's a carefree way to start your day. While waiting in line, you see a magazine headline that your favorite celebrity, Oprah, practices mindfulness. What the heck is mindfulness you wonder?

DEFINING MINDFULNESS

There are many ways to define mindfulness; however, Dr. Jon Kabat-Zinn's definition of mindfulness (1994) most elegantly captures its essence:

> Mindfulness means paying attention in a particular way: On purpose, in the present moment, and non-judgmentally.

Kabat-Zinn is a famous teacher of mindfulness meditation and the founder of the mindfulness-based stress reduction (MBSR) program at the University of Massachusetts Medical Center. MBSR is a mindfulness-based treatment designed to help people with pain and a range of other medical conditions and life stressors that were initially considered difficult to treat in a hospital setting. MBSR will be reviewed later in the book.

In his definition Kabat-Zinn instructs that the task is to pay attention in a particular way, which implies that there are ways of paying attention that are not mindful.

The particular way in which to pay attention has three components:

Paying Attention: On Purpose

The act of mindfulness involves an intentional and conscious decision to focus on our attention or awareness. It is this intentional and purposeful quality of directing our attention that initiates mindful awareness. However, simply being aware is not the same as mindfulness. For instance, if while you are drinking your cup of coffee your boyfriend calls and asks what you are doing, you might say: "Hi! I'm at Starbucks drinking my latte." Clearly you know that you are drinking coffee but that does not mean that you are drinking coffee mindfully.

If, on the other hand, you decided that you were going to do your morning routine slightly differently, and that once you got the coffee you sat down and, with intention, brought all your awareness to the act of drinking your coffee, now you are doing so mindfully. By putting aside all distractions, and even while noting that your phone is ringing—but in this case not answering the call—bringing all your attention to every sensual, emotional, and mental experience of drinking the coffee, you are drinking your coffee mindfully.

Most of us rarely bring such purposeful attention to everyday activities. We tend to live lives of mindless repetition, lives of habitual and predictable responses and behaviors. In many ways this way of interacting with the world is essential. Taking the time to examine every element of every moment would slow things down tremendously, and at times such slowing down would prevent effective participation in the typical pace of life. For instance, imagine that you had to mindfully walk from one classroom to another and slowed down enough to marvel in the miracle that is each and every step. You consider the muscles in motion, the sensation of your foot on the floor, and the coordination and brain activity that go into each step. If you were to mindfully take one step after another through total awareness of such movement, you would likely be late to class, that is, if you ever made it there at all. However, there is a difference between mindless walking and mindful walking, between mindless coffee drinking and mindful coffee drinking: the first qualitative difference is that mindful attention is done purposefully and intentionally.

Let's take the example of your coffee drinking. When you are purposefully aware of drinking your coffee, you are intentionally bringing all of your attention to the act and process of drinking. You deliberately notice the sensations, the tastes, and the textures of the coffee as it enters your mouth. You notice your responses to those experiences. When you notice your mind wandering to other topics, or hear your phone ringing, you notice that your mind has wandered and that you have heard your phone ringing and then gently bring your full attention to the drinking of your coffee.

If you were drinking the coffee mindlessly, you would be drinking while chatting to the baristas, thinking about your final semester at school, talking to your boyfriend, or doing many other things, without specifically concentrating on drinking the coffee.

This purposefulness is a very important part of mindfulness. Having the intention of staying with the current experience as it unfolds begins to train the brain in mindful awareness.

Paying Attention: In the Present Moment

By its nature, the mind tends to wander, and this is because the brain produces thoughts. The brain has 100 trillion neural connections. This is a huge number. If you wanted to count to 100 trillion and could count to 100 in one second, it would take 32,000 years to get to the end. And with so many neural connections, there is a lot of brain activity, although most of it is not in our awareness. Just as the stomach produces stomach juices, the brain produces thoughts. The mind tends to wander all over the place and through all kinds of thoughts, imaginations, fantasies, and responses. Most of these thoughts are transient and never reach our awareness. Some thoughts feel more significant, in that they are attached to emotions—including thoughts paired with anger, deep desire, revenge, and jealousy. As we dwell on these kinds of thoughts, we strengthen the connection of the thought with the emotions, and the tightening of this pairing, especially with difficult emotions, can cause suffering. Mostly, suffering thoughts are those about the past or future, and yet the past no longer exists and the future is simply a story we tell ourselves until it happens, and it might not be the story we created. The one moment we actually can experience—the present moment—is often the one that seems the most elusive.

And so with mindfulness the task is to notice what is going on right now. This does not mean no longer thinking about the past or future, but it does mean that if the past or future comes to mind, then a thought about the yesterday is labeled as a "past thought" being had in the present moment and a thought about tomorrow is labeled as a "future thought" being had in the present moment.

Paying Attention: Nonjudgmentally

The adjective "judgmental" is typically used in the context of the formation of opinions—typically critical ones—about an experience. A judgmental opinion is usually not derived from curiosity or open mindedness and is often one of condemnation. Paying attention nonjudgmentally means accepting the current moment, and everything in it, as a point in time in a constant flow of changing moments. The idea is that by letting go of critical judgments, in other words letting go of the idea that things should be other than what they are or that they should be the way we want or wish them to be, the mind becomes more skilled at recognizing that we don't really have much, if any, control over any given moment. The task at hand is to simply observe without thinking or evaluating. Not judging means not labeling the experience as good or bad. Or, if a judgment arises, mindfulness is noticing the judgment as judgment and then letting go of it. Mindfulness is noticing being upset if you are experiencing something you don't want to be experiencing or not experiencing something you would rather be experiencing. It is acceptance of what arises, bringing full attention to the experience of this moment and then moving on to the next experience without holding on to the past moment. It is accepting whatever arises, as it arises. By doing so you recognize that moments start, end, and then no longer are. Whether an experience is desirable or painful, mindfulness treats it by noticing it without judging it.

Another final element to mindfulness not explicitly included in Kabat-Zinn's definition is that mindfulness is a nonreactive state. This means that a thought as it arises is neither expressed nor repressed but simply observed. For example, you notice a good friend whispering into your girlfriend's ear. You notice the emotion of jealousy arise and have the thought that she is cheating on you and that you should confront her. Nonreactive mindfulness notices the thoughts and emotions as they form. Expressing the thought by confronting your girlfriend and accusing her of cheating on you would not be mindful. Repressing your thoughts by telling yourself that you are being ridiculous, or that you shouldn't be having such thoughts, would not be consistent with the practice of mindfulness. A mindful stance would be the noticing of the emotion of jealousy and noticing of the thought of wanting to confront. The benefit to nonreactivity is that it slows the practitioner down to the point that any ensuing decision as to what to do will be based on a more open-minded and curious perspective and will be less emotionally driven.

2. Why is mindfulness relevant?

For decades students and workers have been urged to slow down and de-stress. Long work shifts and mountains of homework have led to a marked increase in anxiety and high blood pressure and over the long term high rates of heart disease, depression, and stroke. The long-term consequences of unrelenting stress can be fatal.

The desire for a better and fuller life for ourselves and for those we love has been around forever, and yet societies' unrelenting insistence on upward mobility is taking its toll. The stress of a nonstop lifestyle is correlated with early death and has led to a sharp increase in suicide. The overall suicide rate rose by 24 percent from 1999 to 2014, according to the National Center for Health Statistics (Curtin, Warner, & Hedegaard, 2016). A 2014 survey by Dr. Robert Gallagher at the University of Pittsburgh that looked at college counseling centers found that more than half of the students asking for help had severe psychological problems, an increase of 13 percent in just two years. The two most common diagnoses in students were anxiety and depression. A report of women in college (Roth, 2003) describes how its female students felt pressure to be "effortlessly perfect": smart, accomplished, fit, beautiful, and popular, all without visible effort. According to a 2015 study by Dr. Cynthia Fontanella at Ohio State University, adolescents in rural America are committing suicide at twice the rate of their urban peers. Mindfulness is one practice that can lead to overall well-being and a lasting reduction in stress.

From very early on, children are forced to focus on the future and what they are going to do. Social media adds to their burden by creating external models for the way they ought to be, points of reference that implicitly and explicitly show whether the child is in or out of his or her social group. And yet children have little choice. They know no better. They have little opportunity to step away from the tsunami of information and social comparisons, and when they don't fit in, stress and anxiety become constant companions. Without an ability to focus on the here and now, there is then no way to develop effective problem-solving skills. Children don't learn to just sit quietly and be mindful, and this can be exacerbated by parents who feel that if their children are doing "nothing," they are falling behind their peer group.

And yet without sitting quietly, they will never have the natural experience of calm. Sometimes when they can't sit still, they are prescribed medication which can lead to unnatural states of calm, and this in turn can lead to a dependence on prescription drugs or substances like alcohol to take the edge off stress. The use of psychiatric drugs by adult Americans increased 22 percent from 2001 to 2010, with one in five adults now taking at least one medication. In 2010, Americans spent more than $11 billion on antidepressants. If these drugs had long-lasting benefit, why aren't we getting better? Why are more people stressed out, and why are suicide rates on the rise?

Without teaching mindful awareness from early on, children miss out on the wellness benefits of knowing their own experience. Ready access to electronic entertainment means that they aren't able to fully immerse themselves in the moment. Gaming and social media companies have learned to hijack and exploit neural circuits and are open in their desire to provide content that rewards a person for spending as much time as possible on their site. When a child experiences the reward of achieving a goal in an interactive electronic media game, neurons in the ventral tegmental area of the midbrain release the neurotransmitter dopamine into the brain's pleasure centers. Dopamine acting on the pleasure centers tells the child that the experience was pleasurable, and this in turn can lead to endless hours of compulsive behavior such as a need to keep playing a game or to constantly check e-mail. These compulsions meet the definition of narrow focused attention but come at the cost of expanded awareness and, over time, impact a person's ability to reliably know his or her emotional self and experience rich interpersonal relationships.

Fortunately, children are not complete slaves to electronics, and schools often provide other social activities such as team sports which foster participation and relationship building, both essential building blocks for mindful awareness. Sadly though for many young children and adolescents, school budget cuts across the nation together with a greater focus on academic performance has led to a reduction or elimination of many school physical education programs. The toll is an incremental impact on mental wellness as well as physical wellness, leading to significant concerns such as the increasing rate of obesity in our young people. Getting young people to start paying attention to their own minds as early as possible can lead to a reversal of the impact of stress and lack of focus in future years.

Mindfulness is relevant because in an era of a ceaseless rise in health-care costs and the increase in psychological suffering underscored by an uptick in suicide rates and numbers of Americans taking psychiatric medications, it offers a cost-effective and enduring option to tackle these ills. In a 2004 research paper by Dr. Scott Bishop and colleagues, the authors reviewed 30 years of mindfulness research, showing that the practice demonstrated significant physical and psychological benefits. These include more positive emotions; greater ability to deal with bad experiences; and reduced stress, anxiety, and depression. These will be reviewed in greater depth later in the book; however, this list will preview the benefits of practicing mindfulness. Mindfulness improves physical and mental health.

Physical benefits include stress reduction, improved heart and cardiovascular health, reduced chronic pain which helps relieve stress, improved immune system, and improved gastrointestinal functioning. Mental benefits include reduced anxiety, worry, and depression; reduced substance abuse; benefit in eating disorders; improved sleep; and improved resilience in the face of difficult situations. Mindfulness also increases overall satisfaction in life, makes it easier to enjoy life's pleasures as they occur, helps the practitioner fully engage in activities, and can enhance relationships.

More and more mindfulness meditation is being combined with various forms of medical therapies as well as psychotherapy, especially cognitive behavioral therapies like dialectical behavior therapy. This makes sense for various reasons. Both meditation and psychotherapy share the goal of helping people gain perspective on repetitive, maladaptive, and self-defeating, sometimes self-destructive, thoughts and behaviors.

3. What is meditation?

The terms "meditation" and "mindfulness" are often used interchangeably, and oftentimes, when writers and teachers talk about mindfulness and meditation, they are, in fact, referring to the same practice. It is not worth getting into a debate as to whether or not they are the same thing, for doing so misses the point. In reality, they are opposite sides of the same coin, but opposite sides nevertheless, and each has its own specific definition and purpose.

Meditation is a technique for stilling the mind and attaining a state of total awareness. It is a practice focused on experiencing our very nature and consciousness. Meditation is not a part of organized religion, even though many religions have meditative practices. It is not concentration, relaxation, loss of control, or any particular kind of physical exercise. It has the goal of developing the capacity to experience the nature of the things around us but more specifically the goal of knowing and experiencing our own nature.

Earlier we described mindfulness as the more narrow practice of non-judgmental focused attention on the present moment. "Meditation" is a broader term that includes a future goal of reaching ultimate consciousness and concentration and, by doing so, developing the capacity to recognize our own mind as it is and in turn the ability to regulate emotions, relationships, thoughts, and experiences. Meditative practices—including mindfulness, yoga, and breathing—hold the promise that with sufficient practice, the meditator will reach a more heightened level of consciousness.

Another major difference is that meditation is a more formal practice. Typically, a meditator sets aside a dedicated time and a dedicated space in order to meditate. The person practicing mindfulness can simply do whatever it is he or she is doing in that moment with mindful awareness and need not necessarily take time out of his or her day to do so. The following analogies may be useful: a religious person attends a formal religious practice on a particular day and at a particular place of worship; however, he or she can also pray whenever he or she wants and needs to necessarily be in a church, temple, or synagogue. A soccer player plays a formal match with his or her team against an opponent on a particular field; however, he or she can choose to juggle the soccer ball on a playground, a gym, or in his or her bedroom, with or without other people present.

Mindfulness tends to be considered as narrower in scope and a way of paying attention to specific experiences like the breath or the drinking of a cup of coffee. Meditation tends to be a more expansive practice and tends to take in the broader context of the experience. It is common during mindfulness practice to be mindful of a specific task and, then when the mind drifts off, to notice the drifting and come back to focusing on the specific task. The meditation's broader goal of attaining heightened consciousness uses the practice of mindfulness as a tool to reach this goal.

The meditation teacher Lodro Rinzler has written that the practice of meditation predates the idea of mindfulness. Long before the Buddha, holy people were meditating; however, the Buddha discovered that the practice of focusing completely on the breath led to a state of mind that facilitated meditation. It was during such a meditative state that he attained enlightenment and the realization of ultimate reality.

In meditation, the meditator tries to attain clarity of mind and get to a state of serenity, relaxation, and inward focus. The idea is that with practice the mind becomes increasingly silent and is therefore no longer a source of distraction, thereby leading to a deepening of the meditative state. It stands to reason why people, whether religious monks in a monastery or lay people seeking stillness of mind, would cloister themselves in a monastery away from the noise of everyday distractions in order to attain such a state.

Although there are differences between the terms "mindfulness" and "meditation," both use very similar techniques to attain a state of self-awareness and self-control, and for the purpose of the questions in the book, the terms will be used interchangeably.

4. What are reasons to practice?

There are many reasons to practice mindfulness, and many of these reasons have been researched and have strong scientific evidence that mindfulness works. The science will be reviewed in greater depth later in this book.

There are emotional, physical, relational, and mental health as well as spiritual health benefits to practicing mindfulness. These benefits compare favorably against contemporary Western approaches to dealing with such issues. This includes, in some circumstances, the use of mindfulness over medication or other medical interventions.

PHYSICAL HEALTH REASONS

Improved Immune Function

Dr. Richie Davidson showed in a study in 2003 that short-term mindfulness training resulted in research participants developing a stronger immune response when challenged with the flu injection.

Protection against DNA Damage

Dr. Elizabeth Blackburn, PhD, looked at the effect of mindfulness on telomerase, a body enzyme that serves to protect DNA from age- and stress-related damage. She showed that people who are regular meditators have improved telomerase function.

Improved Sleep

Research shows that people with chronic insomnia—difficulty sleeping—who practice mindfulness spend less time awake at night, feel more relaxed before going to bed, and have overall less disruption in their sleep. Also even after only eight weeks of practice, when the research participants were examined six months later, the insomnia sufferers had maintained a better quality of sleep.

Reduced Stress Eating

Researchers at UCSF (University of California, San Francisco) studied 30 minutes of mindfulness and then mindful eating on a group of women to see if they could prevent overeating. They did not prescribe a diet, only mindfulness. In the group that didn't practice mindfulness, the control group gained weight. The mindfulness group maintained their weight and lowered their cortisol levels. Cortisol is a stress hormone that leads to many health problems, including an increase in abdominal fat.

Less Physical Pain

Dr. Kabat-Zinn, the developer of MBSR, has shown in multiple studies that mindfulness significantly reduces pain symptoms and improves quality of life in chronic pain patients. Some recent research showed that even after four days of mindfulness training, people reported less pain intensity and discomfort. This research was mirrored by brain scans, which showed reductions in pain-induced brain activity during meditation sessions.

EMOTIONAL HEALTH REASONS

Parts of the Brain Correlated to Positive Emotion Are Activated

Research shows that people who suffer from depression have more brain activity on the right side of their brain, compared to people who have a more positive attitude in life. Happier people tend to have more activity on the left side of their brain. Studies show that in people with depression who practice regular mindfulness, the electrical brain activity begins to shift from right to left and with that comes an increase in overall happiness.

Reduced Likelihood of Depression Returning

A study by Teasdale and Segal showed that people who had suffered from depression who practiced mindfulness could reduce the rate of another episode of depression by up to 44 percent. This effect is similar to that of a person taking regular antidepressant medication.

Less Anxiety

Research by Harvard's Dr. Elizabeth Hoge found that mindfulness practice helped people with generalized anxiety disorder.

OTHER MENTAL HEALTH REASONS

Growth in Higher-Functioning Regions of the Brain

Research by Dr. Sara Lazar, at Harvard University, showed that regular mindfulness was associated with growth in the thickness of the prefrontal cortex, an area of the brain responsible for, among other things, focused attention and emotion regulation. Her research suggested that mindfulness led to reduced age-related brain decline.

Less Burnout

Mindfulness reduces employee stress and burnout. A study of mindfulness on teachers who work at a school for children with severe behavioral problems showed that they had less stress, less depression, and less burnout than teachers who did not meditate.

RELATIONAL HEALTH REASONS

Lasting Harmony

Researchers from UCSF compared 82 female teachers, all married or living with a partner to a control group that hadn't learned meditation. The meditators showed fewer negative facial expressions during a marital interaction test. This was an important finding because people who demonstrate negative facial expressions toward their partners are more likely to get divorced.

Increasing Satisfaction

Research from Maharishi International University in Iowa found that women who practiced regular meditation reported significantly greater marital satisfaction than those who didn't and that the more regular the mindfulness practice, the greater the marital satisfaction.

Less Loneliness

Research shows that loneliness among the elderly can be dangerous, as it raises risks for a number of health conditions. A study from University of California, Los Angeles, found that mindfulness practice helped the elderly decrease feelings of loneliness as well as boost their overall health.

SPIRITUAL HEALTH

Increased Experience of Awe

Research by Dr. Brian Ostafin at the University of Groningen looked at the relationship between mindfulness and awe—two of the core elements of many spiritual traditions. Prior to viewing awe-inspiring images, half of the study group listened to a 10-minute mindfulness audio recording, while the other half listened to non-mindfulness control audio. Participants who listened to the mindfulness tapes experienced a greater awe reaction than the group who didn't in response to the awe-provoking images.

The practice of mindfulness continues to undergo rigorous scientific research. All the research is providing evidence as to its utility and giving us many health and other reasons to do the practice.

5. Is mindfulness the same as yoga or relaxation?

Many people associate mindfulness meditation with yoga, stress reduction, and relaxation, and although some people who practice mindfulness also practice yoga and find that through mindfulness they are less stressed and more relaxed, these are different practices. From a Western perspective, yoga and meditation are almost synonymous; however, although these two are related, they are different concepts.

The word "yoga" is an ancient Sanskrit word, which means "union," and in its original form meant the union between a person's soul and the spirit or the rest of the universe. For many, yoga is associated with physical exercises only, and in that context perfecting the postures, known as *asanas*, body positions that are familiar to anyone who thinks about the term "yoga." And yet for devout practitioners, the physical postures are only the most superficial component of a journey that delves into the infinite depths and possibilities of the human mind, body, and soul. The idea was that through an eight-step yoga practice a person could attain the union between all aspects of personhood. The eight steps are as follows:

1. What you do: Be pure in body and mind, self-disciplined, contemplative, and devoted to practice.
2. What you don't do: Don't hurt others, don't lie, don't steal, and don't desire.
3. The physical positions: Practice by establishing the correct posture in each position.

4. Breath control: Through awareness of each breath.
5. The withdrawal of senses: Focusing on inward experiences rather external sensations.
6. Concentration: By holding the mind on one thought.
7. Meditation: By holding in the mind the expansiveness of everything.
8. Spiritual ecstasy: By recognizing the unity of self and the universe.

And so mindfulness meditation is one component of yoga. To get to the condition where a person is more likely to be in a mindful state, the practices of relaxing the body, calming the mind, and controlling the breath are common to both yoga and meditation.

Mindfulness and yoga are typically considered to be different yet complementary paths into the end goal of living wisely. For some on this journey, the focus of attention is on their body and for others on observing the stillness in long stretches of sitting quietly.

Jon Kabat-Zinn recognized that yoga has the potential to help reverse the effects of a sedentary lifestyle on the muscle system and in particular for those who have chronic pain and illness. Because his research had already shown the benefits of meditation on a broad range of health conditions, the idea of combining yoga with meditation was seen as a way of integrating different aspects and virtues of the mental and physical practices.

As Kabat-Zinn describes it, when clinic patients integrated meditation and yoga practices into their treatment, and these were patients who suffered from a wide range of chronic disorders and diseases, the result was an enduring improvement in many measures of health. It was this combination that then evolved into the eight-week course, now known as mindfulness-based stress reduction (MBSR).

DIFFERENT FORMS

There are various paths of yoga that lead toward the goal of spiritual, mental, and physical union. Each is a branch of one comprehensive system (www.yogananda-srf.org):

Hatha yoga—a system of physical postures, whose higher purpose is to purify the body, attaining an awareness and control over its internal states and rendering it fit for meditation.

Karma yoga—selfless service to others as part of one's larger self, without attachment to the results.

Mantra yoga—centering the consciousness within through the repetition of certain universal root-word sounds.

> Bhakti yoga—all-surrendering devotion through which a person strives to see and love the divinity in every creature and in everything, thus maintaining an unceasing worship.
>
> Gyana yoga—the path of wisdom, which emphasizes the application of discriminative intelligence to achieve spiritual liberation.
>
> Raja yoga—the royal or highest path of yoga, which combines the essence of all the other paths.

The physical practice of yoga and the observing practice of sitting still in meditative contemplation are complementary skill sets that deepen the experience of self and universal awareness.

6. What is enlightenment?

Enlightenment has philosophical, religious, and secular definitions. When it comes to mindfulness, the idea is one of awakening, meaning that a person is awakened to his or her true nature. It is a state of awareness in which all things and experiences are recognized as they are without being influenced by time, space, thoughts, emotions, or words.

In 1784, the philosopher Immanuel Kant said that Enlightenment is "man's emergence from his self-imposed *nonage*." He defined nonage as the inability to use our own understanding without another person's guidance. He argued that using books, religious clergy, physicians, and other people to determine what to do in life means that you are not using your own intellectual ability. He further argued that this nonage was self-imposed and urged people to *sapere aude* or "dare to know." To have "the courage to use your own understanding," is, as he described, "the motto of the enlightenment." This courage means to work against the comfort of living a life guided by others rather than by using our own inherent understanding.

In Kant's definition the overlap with the Buddhist concept of awareness is clear as Kant's philosophy compels people to challenge the idea that understanding comes from the outside of ourselves.

From a historical perspective the Age of Enlightenment started somewhere between 1650 and 1700. It arose in France and England when certain intellectuals considered themselves as "enlightened" in comparison with most other people and in turn set out to "enlighten" the unenlightened. They considered themselves enlightened, in that they used reason, logic, and science to free themselves from ignorance, dogma, and superstition and, in particular, to free themselves from the Catholic dogma of the day. The secular enlightenment did not mean that the enlightened were atheists but instead argued that certain beliefs central to Catholicism were historical artifacts and that because these tenets had been created by people, rather than the divine, the dogmas belonged in the realm of fiction.

In Catholicism, the enlightenment movement began in the late 15th and early 16th centuries and was a reaction to its fall into corruption and chaos. Some left the church altogether, the Protestants, but others sought to reform the church. Leading Catholic thinkers promoted religious freedom and tolerance, defended the rights and participation of women in broad areas of secular and religious life, challenged superstition, and recognized advances in biblical scholarship. They opened themselves to the idea that science and economics had important contributions to make. The views and proposals of these enlightened Catholics were often vigorously challenged by the conservative wings of the church; however, over time, reform-minded popes integrated their ideas into Catholic teaching.

Jewish enlightenment, also known as *the Haskalah* (Schumacher-Brunhes, 2012), was an intellectual movement among the Jews of Central and Eastern Europe. It arose during the 1770s and ended with the rise of Jewish nationalism. It sought to preserve the Jews as a separate group and focused on reviving Hebrew for secular purposes, including the use of the language in the contemporary press and literature. At the same time it worked toward an integration of Jews within non-Jewish communities and focused on including the study of non-Jewish perspectives, and the adoption of more secular customs and style of clothing and appearance. At its core, and like its Catholic counterpart, Jewish enlightenment promoted rational thinking, liberalism, freedom of thought, and enquiry.

From a Buddhist perspective, enlightenment is coming to the realization that things are as they are. It is the awe-inspiring awareness of the interconnectedness of things and the experience of the mind at work in relation to the rest of everything. Enlightenment is the moment where a person recognizes that there is no separation between things because they all influence each other. For instance, the heart and the liver are considered different organs but they are parts of the more complex whole, and they cannot exist without each other as they need each of their capacities to be as they are.

All definitions of enlightenment, whether secular, philosophical, or religious, challenge the contemporary orthodoxy and compel the one to be enlightened to contemplate alternatives and examine the habitual nature of one's existence within the natural context. In order to do this, all such examinations require developing an awareness of mindless repetition.

7. Are there different types of meditation?

The practice of mindfulness, which has no goal other than nonjudgmental awareness, always plays a role in meditation, but meditation, which has the particular goal of developing increasing concentration, is not necessarily a part of mindfulness. There are different types of meditation which approach mindfulness qualitatively differently.

A way to clarify the nuances between the meditation practices is to think about the different ways of meditating. Broadly, there are four main types of practices and these are

- concentrative,
- generative,
- receptive, and
- reflective.

These are designations derived from scientific research based on the description of modern meditation teachers who draw on various traditions.

CONCENTRATIVE MEDITATION

The goal of this practice is to focus attention, and typically the practitioner uses some object on which to place his or her attention. The most basic, and yet fundamental, of practices is the focus on the natural rhythm of the breath; nevertheless, any of the senses can be used. And so the person might use a candle flame to look at, a singing bowl to listen to, a raisin to taste, and so on. The objective is to slowly bring all attention to the object or task and with that to calm the attention, unperturbed by other distractions.

Although the focused practice can be as simple as listening to a sound, concentrative meditation can get more complex; for instance, in Tibetan tantric Buddhism, a meditation tradition is to visualize intricate images of Buddha forms and then recite mantras.

Here is a common version of focused breath practice:

- Initially the instruction to the meditator is to follow the breath as it enters and leaves the body and then count each breath after the out-breath.
- After the first breath the person counts "one," after the second "two," and so on until the person reaches ten and then begins again at one.

- Once the person finds that he or she can do this without being distracted, the next step is to count before the breath and again reach 10.
- Next the meditator stops counting and simply attends to the sensations of the air entering and leaving the body.
- Finally, the person focuses attention on the tip of the nose or on the lips at the point when the air comes into contact with the skin.

GENERATIVE MEDITATION

In the West the best-known practice in generative practice is the development of *loving kindness* meditation also known as *metta*. The meditator develops an attitude of loving kindness using images of people in their life as well as awareness of physical sensations.

Here is an example of loving kindness practice:

- In stage one of *metta* you focus on yourself and in your mind say a phrase such as "may I be well and happy, may I be at peace." This is repeated over and over.
- In stage two you focus on a good friend or beloved family member and similarly use the loving kindness phrase toward that person.
- In stage three *metta* is directed toward someone who is a casual acquaintance.
- In stage four it is directed toward someone you dislike or with whom you are having a difficult time.
- Finally, the practice brings *metta* to all four people at once, that is, yourself, the beloved, the neutral person, and the enemy.

Another example of generative meditation is tonglen—the Buddhist practice of breathing in the suffering of others and breathing out love and peace for those suffering with the goal of cultivating compassion.

RECEPTIVE MEDITATION

In the space between concentrative and generative meditation the meditator can also attend to and be receptive of whatever experience is arising. There is an attitude of open receptive awareness as the focus of the receptive type of meditation practice.

Better-known examples of this type of meditation are practices like *zazen* or "just sitting," which is part of the Japanese Zen tradition. The task is to sit calmly, aware of what is happening in your entire experience, with all the senses at play and without judging, following thoughts or try-ing to change the experience. This type of practice is typically done with eyes open, thereby allowing visual stimuli to be part of the experience. More than the other practices, the practitioner gains the significance of being in the present moment.

REFLECTIVE MEDITATION

Reflective meditation is the practice of repeatedly turning attention to a theme and concern but then being open to the thoughts, emotions, and sensations that arise from the experience. As the meditator becomes more experienced in this practice, meditations can include reflection on the impermanence of things and interconnectedness of all things.

8. When is focused attention *not* mindfulness?

A 16-year-old spends eight hours in front of his TV monitor playing a video game. He does not respond to the call for dinner, the need to do his homework, nor to the fact that it is 2:00 in the morning and that he needs to be up at 6:30 to get ready for school. There is no question that all his attention is focused on the game. Is his focused attention on video-playing mindfulness? The answer depends on his state of overall awareness.

Mindlessness is the state of being so lost in an experience, be it thought or emotion, that you become almost completely unaware of the things outside of that experience. At any given point awareness lies somewhere between mindlessness and mindfulness, and for most of us, the majority of what we do is on the mindless side of the curve.

This is because it is easy for the mind to get so used to our surroundings and other people that we stop noticing them altogether. Without paying attention with full awareness it can become a habit to be so focused on completing a task or finishing a video game that you miss everything else happening around you. Whether or not you realize it, most of your life is a set of behaviors done mindlessly. There is great benefit to such mindless-ness. Paying too much attention to each and every step of every action would slow that action down; nevertheless, this mindlessness can become so habitual that little is done with attentive awareness.

Therefore, if the 16-year-old is completely unaware of the call for dinner, the need to do homework, and the time of night, then the video-playing is a mindless activity even though he is using his brain. This is not to say that the activity is useless, and studies have shown that for people who play video games, the ability to master fast-moving scenes on the screen in order to achieve a goal improves focused attention, and this can be particularly helpful to older people whose ability to pay attention can decline as they age.

If the 16-year-old said to himself "I am, with intention, going to focus on simply playing the video game, noticing my experience without judgment and being effective—in that he also does what he needs to do like going to dinner and finishing his homework—and while I am playing the game, I will not multi-task, will not also be on social media, and when my thoughts wander from the game, I will notice them wandering and get back to the game," then he would be playing the game mindfully.

Although paying attention is a component of mindfulness, it does not embody all of what mindfulness is.

The act of paying attention is the behavior of carefully focusing on, while listening to and thinking about someone or something. What is different between this action and the practice of mindfulness is that mindfulness includes the intentional awareness that you are paying attention. It is a prerequisite to learning and for many teachers and students an essential component to classroom management and student motivation, and yet for a large minority of students, paying attention to the focus of the classroom subject matter is not easy due to difficulty concentrating because of suffering from significantly interfering disruptive brain conditions such as attention deficit disorder, learning disabilities, and dyslexia.

From a developmental perspective, the brain's attentional system evolved to quickly recognize and respond to danger and to ignore situations where change is gradual and that don't immediately threaten the person, and this has an impact on school learning. Because academics tend to be nonthreatening and relatively slow paced in their didactic curricula, it can be difficult for some children and particularly those with disabilities to concentrate fully on the classroom material. Training brain through mindfulness practices enhances attentional abilities and further develops a person's ability to more effectively use his or her capacity to focus on what is contextually relevant, as in sitting in a classroom or not playing video games at the expense of completing homework or having dinner with family.

9. Isn't mindfulness just a fad that will come and go?

It is understandable that some people consider mindfulness a fad. These days it is endorsed by famous athletes, celebrities, and business leaders. These are not people who look like the meditating sages of ancient times, commonly depicted paintings, and textbooks. And so of the celebrities and athletes who don't have countless hours meditating and yet are strong proponents of mindfulness, aren't they too buying into the hype? The world has always looked for quick fixes to complicated psychological problems, and so self-help books abound. Is mindfulness simply not the current attempt to address the stress of everyday life and, as with other such attempts, it too will pass when the next "thing" comes along?

A review of the various definitions of the word "fad" leads to a consensus understanding that a fad is a widely shared enthusiasm for something and that the enthusiasm for the thing is short lived. The excitement for fad tends to have little to do with the intrinsic value of whatever the thing is. For instance, there was a time when beanie babies, a small stuffed animal toy, were a fad. People were obsessed with the toys and drove up their price until no one was interested anymore and the toys quickly became valueless. Things that are not a fad are things with utility and practicality. Obviously things like drinking water and oxygen are essential and not transient in use. Language is not a fad. Cooking is not a fad. All have enduring use and have endured for millennia.

With regard to mental and physical wellness, a current fad is the use of psychiatric diagnoses to include a broad range of people who would not historically have been included as having a mental condition. Another fad is the use of untested psychotherapies. Typically, the best way to address a fad is to stay away from the frenzy that arises and from a mental health perspective to stay away from untested ideas and instead to use an evidence-based approach. It is in this context that many argue that mindfulness is a fad.

The argument goes that suddenly mindfulness seems to be everywhere. They point out that news headlines and research studies exalt the use of mindfulness and that the sudden surge in popularity makes it a fad by definition.

It makes sense that some are skeptical. Mindfulness is being used for sports, to help people with anger, to stop smoking and drinking, to reduce the effects of cancer, to lower aggression, to reduce stress and pain, to increase happiness, and so on.

One of the major criticisms of the practice of mindfulness is that large enterprises like the *Huffington Post*, Google, and Aetna might be teaching it to employees as a quick fix for reducing their stress and increasing their productivity and that this approach is "fad-like." Certainly, a one-day seminar on mindfulness would not be what is called for. Providing workers with a regular and consistent way to handle the stress of the workplace while potentially improving their overall happiness, productivity, and relationships is beneficial to the whole company. It is the reason that so many companies encourage and provide the space and time to practice mindfulness.

Relatively, mindfulness is a brand new idea in the West, and yet this Eastern concept has led to overall health benefits and wellness in many, and as a consequence an ever-increasing number of people want to know more and adopt it as a way of enhancing their lives. Because of this it is not a fad, and there is no indication that it will go away anytime soon. Mindfulness may not be the next cure-all panacea. The core principles of mindfulness were developed almost 2,500 years ago, and the tome *The Path to Purification* was written by Buddhaghosa 1,500 years ago. These principles were brought to Western medicine by Jon Kabat-Zinn, whose books *Wherever You Go, There You Are*, and *Full Catastrophe Living* became best sellers. His approach based on mindfulness, known as mindfulness-based stress reduction (MBSR) program, has helped countless patients and been shown to be effective in many research studies. The basic premise was that for people who had chronic pain and who had failed multiple different pain treatments, fighting the suffering led to even more suffering because the person dealt not only with the pain but also with the agony that comes from wishing that the pain were not as it is. Learning to accept the pain mindfully led many to experience reduced suffering.

And so the main reason that it is not a fad is that science has shown that mindfulness taps into the fundamental way that the brain works. Just because we might not know the exact way that exercise enhances muscle function does not mean that exercise is a fad. The health benefits of regular exercise are not only scientifically validated but also subjectively experienced by many. Similarly, not knowing exactly how mindfulness works on the various parts of the brain does not mean that the scientific evidence is useless.

Skeptics will remain, and yet there are many doubters who have experienced what many meditators have known for thousands of years: that is, that with mindfulness the overall quality of their emotional, professional, and relational lives improves with consistent practice.

How to Practice Mindfulness

10. Can anyone practice?

Anyone can practice mindfulness. If you can breathe, you can be mindful because the breath and the ability to focus on the breath is always with you. The main reason people say that they are unable to do mindfulness is a lack of persistence. By setting aside a few minutes each day to focus on the breath and gradually increasing the amount of time focusing, mindfulness becomes increasingly easier. That is true of all behaviors and actions. Repetition makes the task more familiar and more effortless.

DOES AGE MATTER?

Children often pay more attention to the present moment than adults do. When they are very young, they don't typically get caught up in holding onto past hurts. In part it is because they don't have a sense of others' motivations, and so they don't spend a lot of time thinking about others' intentions. Also young children don't have significant obligations, and so thinking about starting to prepare for dinner or what clothes to wear the next day or what they are going to say to their boss is not part of their life. As children get older, their responsibilities increase, and they have to do things that get them into habitual living such as getting ready for school, making sure they have packed their snack, and being on time for the bus. The fact that they are more present in their living is closer to mindfulness but is different from mindfulness, in that there is typically no awareness or intentionality to being present. Nevertheless, mindfulness comes easier to young children because the "being present" and the "without judgment" aspects of mindfulness are already there.

Most of the research on mindfulness focuses on the practice in adults. Very few studies have been done on the use of mindfulness with children aged 5–12, even though many schools are including mindful moments in their daily curriculum. Australian educator Nicole Albrecht (2015) estimates that there are now more than 30 different mindfulness programs around the world. The research on mindfulness in schools for younger students is scant, although there appears to be an improvement in academic performance, attention, and feelings of connectedness with others, it is unclear if these improvements endure and so further research is needed. All of the studies suggest that children appear to enjoy the practice of mindfulness, with the major concern being that some find the quiet exploration of the mind to be anxiety provoking. Because of this, most school-based mindfulness programs incorporate focusing on the breath while doing some activity.

Different from research in the young, there is plenty of research on mindfulness in older people and the benefits of the practice. These include the following:

Improves longevity: A 1989 study found that elderly practitioners of transcendental meditation, a type of mindfulness, lived longer than the comparison group. The study followed a large number of seniors living in different homes for the elderly and found a significant decrease in death rates among those who meditate. Another way that meditation increases longevity is that it has been shown to slow the natural aging of cells.

Decreases loneliness: It has also been demonstrated that the practices of mindfulness and meditation decrease loneliness and increase feelings of connectedness. According to one UCLA (University of California, Los Angeles) study, seniors who engaged in a simple eight-week meditation program showed significant decreases in the rates of self-reported loneliness. Since isolation is a major issue among older adults, such results are promising.

May slow Alzheimer's dementia: A 2013 study showed that mindfulness meditation could slow the progression of Alzheimer's disease. The researchers hypothesized that mindfulness protected the brain against anxiety and stress, symptoms which are known to worsen Alzheimer's symptoms.

Reduces health-care costs: A 2005 study by psychologist Robert Herron found that seniors who practiced meditation had significantly fewer hospitalizations. The researchers found that in comparison to the group that did not meditate, the meditators "five-year cumulative reduction in payments to physicians was 70% less than the control group [non-meditating group]."

Less depression: A 2014 Thai study added meditation to walking therapy for seniors. The researchers found that seniors who practiced meditation had significantly less depression than seniors who only participated in the walking group.

Their caregivers benefit: A 2013 UCLA study studied the effects of yoga on caregivers of people with different forms of dementia including Alzheimer's and found that caregivers practiced "a brief, simple daily meditation reduced the stress levels of people who care for those stricken by Alzheimer's and dementia."

DOES RELIGION MATTER?

Mindfulness has its origins in contemplative practices that go back many thousands of years. Buddhism, Hinduism, and other religions that predate Christianity, Judaism, and Islam have been practicing various forms of mindfulness as integral to their religion. To this day almost all religions have mindful contemplative practices: there is Catholic centering prayer, Buddhist meditation, the Jewish Kabbalah, and Sufi mysticism in Islam.

Many nonreligious philosophies include elements of mindfulness. The writings of Epictetus and Marcus Aurelius speak to an approach to life that is very consistent with mindful living. Whether religious, atheist, or secular, all people breathe, and the practice of observing the breath belongs to no religious or philosophical tradition, and therefore, people of all faiths can practice mindfulness. They can choose to do it as a spiritual practice or not.

DOES PHYSICAL HEALTH MATTER?

People can practice mindfulness irrespective of their state of health, and in fact, the developers of mindfulness-based stress reduction (MBSR) have treated more than 20,000 people and over the past 35 years "shown consistent, reliable, and reproducible demonstrations of major and clinically relevant reductions in medical and psychological symptoms across a wide range of medical diagnoses, including many different chronic pain conditions, other medical diagnoses and in medical patients with a secondary diagnosis of anxiety and/or panic, over the eight weeks of the MBSR intervention, and maintenance of these changes in some cases for up to four years of follow-up" (Center for Mindfulness).

11. How do you practice mindfulness?

As with any other practice, mindfulness is a skill that can be learned. Mindfulness meditation is an intentional practice, meaning that it is not something that you stumble on. Deciding to do so is the same as deciding to practice playing piano or to go for a walk. However, simply watching a Zen monk or Yogi sitting still does not say much about what it is that they are doing. In meditation, learning how to be still and focused on the task at hand is the first step. The process of cultivating stillness begins with the breath: observing air flowing in and then air flowing out. This is the beginning, and the rest of the skill practice can be further broken down.

WHAT TO DO

The "what to do" of mindfulness has been broken down into three easy-to-follow steps by Dr. Marsha Linehan, the developer of dialectical behavior therapy (DBT) (1993). She called these skills the "what skills," and they are practices of observing, describing, and participating.

Observe means to notice everything in the environment, including thoughts, emotions, feelings, and sensations *without reacting* to them. It is the practice of seeing things as they are and allowing experiences to come and go without trying to control them. Observing means not pushing any experience away no matter how enjoyable no painful it is. It is being alert to all experiences through all senses and doing so without putting words to the experience.

After observing, the next step is to use words to describe the experience. It is the individual experience because even though people may have similar experiences, the perspective of each one is influenced by multiple factors. Describing means using words to represent the facts of the situation; for instance, "the flower is blue," "the time is 12:35," "I am feeling angry." It means staying away from judgments or opinions, unless you explicitly state your opinion or assumption as your own, as a part of describing your experience of the event.

Participating means throwing yourself fully into your experience. It means doing so without needing to love or hate the experience. It is practicing being in each moment as it comes without getting caught up in every detail of the experience and without becoming self-conscious. It is engaging in the moment and practicing letting go of thoughts like "how am I doing?" or "how do I look?" or "others must think I'm ridiculous."

HOW TO DO IT

The "how to do" of mindfulness is also described by Linehan in DBT who called these skills the "how skills," and they are practices of being one-mindful, nonjudgmental, and effective.

One-mindfully means focusing on one thing at a time. It is the opposite of multitasking, a common habit in contemporary society. The idea is to do one thing in the moment and do that thing without distraction. When speaking on the phone, just speak on the phone. Don't also be answering e-mails or watching TV. The ability to focus on one thing trains the mind to let go of distractions.

Being nonjudgmental is the practice of taking a nonjudgmental stance. This means leaving out automatic labels such as "good" or "bad," "ugly" or "beautiful," and any other adjective that automatically stops curiosity and further exploration of whatever is being judged. As such, there are no good thoughts and emotions or bad thoughts and emotions. They are all recognized as equal experiential phenomena. Then, when judgments arise, they are noted and labeled as such: "I am having a judgment about my thought," "I am judging my thought as 'bad,'" and so on.

To be effective means to do what needs to be done. It means being effective over being "right." It is the practice of becoming aware of the space between thought and action, which in turn leads to reduced impulsivity and behavior that can be destructive. It is noting the apparent righteousness of a perspective or thought and then noting whether acting on the thought is the effective thing to do.

SHOULD EYES BE OPEN OR SHUT?

Both methods are common. Historically, because monasteries were dark places, the monks and nuns practicing meditation were likely to fall asleep if they closed their eyes. Keeping eyes open helped to prevent them falling asleep. Another reason to keep eyes open is that most of life is lived with eyes open, and it is important to learn mindfulness that way.

The case for eyes closed is that contemporary life bombards us with external stimuli and that it is difficult not to be distracted by these. By keeping eyes closed we shut down one sensory channel of incoming stimuli. But Master Deshimaru adds a reason for closing our eyes, and it is related to occidental culture.

SITTING AND CULTIVATING STILLNESS

The most common practice is sitting on the floor. It is considered the most stable position; however, because of physical constraints, injury, or illness, some practice mindfulness by lying down or standing. Sitting on the ground is recommended as it is considered the most stable position. For those who can, the most common practice is sitting cross-legged in the lotus position. Alternatively, many use a small pillow or folded-over blanket to raise the buttocks just a little, and then with the buttocks on the pillow the knees kneel on the ground so that the knees can touch the ground. With your bottom on the pillow and two knees touching the ground, a stable tripod base is formed. Whether the lotus or kneeling position, hands are placed gently on the lap or on the thighs.

Because of physical limitation, some find it easier to meditate by sitting on a chair. The posture then is sitting with feet on the floor, with back straight and erect, and with shoulders loose and relaxed. Once the position is established, mindfulness practice begins by noticing the breath.

Sitting meditation is useful but not essential. It is a great way to start practicing and to establish a routine; however, any task and physical posture can be experienced with mindful awareness.

IS THERE A GOOD TIME OF DAY TO PRACTICE?

Any time of day is a good time to practice; however, because the demands of daily life, including work, school, and family, often require that obligations be met, taking time first thing in the morning, before the busyness of life takes over, can be the most reliable time of day to find 10 minutes. Ten minutes is about the time needed to open up a computer and start reading e-mails or making a cup of coffee or walking half a mile. For some people, using 10 minutes of a lunch break at work, or recess at school to do a mindful walk or sit mindfully in a park or in the office, is more convenient.

12. What is a meditation retreat?

There are many different forms of retreats; however, all share the idea of taking a dedicated amount of time during which a person stops his or her daily routine to focus on the practice of mindfulness. Typically, a retreat takes place in a tranquil, often rural, environment away from distracting electronics, traffic, and crowds. In Europe and Asia, ancient monasteries commonly open up some of their space to allow for the secular practice of meditation.

WHAT DOES IT LOOK LIKE?

Retreats vary greatly in what they offer, and *retreatants*—persons attending a retreat—can often choose something that matches their needs. Typical offerings are a focus on yoga, silent mindfulness, loving compassion, positive psychology, happiness, healthy eating, and spirituality. For instance:

> *Silent retreat:* One of the best-known meditation retreats is a silent retreat known as *Vipassana*. Typically it lasts between 3 and 10 days. During the time, retreatants are not allowed to speak, read, write, listen to music, or engage in any other form of engagement with the outside world. Ordinarily women and men sleep in different quarters and are segregated. The food is typically vegetarian, and in some retreats only fruits and vegetables are allowed to be eaten after breakfast.
> A typical schedule is:

4:00 a.m.	Morning wake-up bell
4:30–6:30 a.m.	Sitting meditation in the hall with 5-minute walks after every 30 minutes of sitting
6:30–8:00 a.m.	Mindful eating of breakfast with post-breakfast chores
8:00–11:00 a.m.	Sitting meditation in the hall with 5-minute walks after every 30 minutes of sitting
11:00–12:00	Mindful eating of lunch with post-lunch chores
12:00–1:00 p.m.	Post-chore rest
1:00–5:00 p.m.	Sitting meditation in the hall with 5-minute walks after every 30 minutes of sitting
5:00–6:00 p.m.	Mindful tea break
6:00–7:00 p.m.	Sitting meditation in the hall with 5-minute walks after every 30 minutes of sitting
7:00–8:15 p.m.	Teacher's lecture in the hall
8:15–9:30 p.m.	Sitting meditation in the hall with 5-minute walks after every 30 minutes of sitting
9:30 p.m.	Retire to your room and lights out

Loving compassion retreat: Metta is another word for friendship or lovingkindness and on retreat is taught as a meditation that cultivates a person's capacity for an open and loving heart. The focus is on meditative practices that increase levels of compassion as well as joy in the happiness of others. The realization is that the person so practicing increases his or her own capacity for joy, concentration, and fearlessness, and develops a greater ability to love.

Yoga retreat: The focus of this kind of retreat is on yoga as a way into meditation.

Positive psychology retreat: This kind of retreat explores the neuroscience and introduces the practice, leading optimal functioning through the practice of positive psychology, which is the focus on the strengths and virtues that enable people, communities, and organizations to thrive and prosper.

Mindful eating retreat: These retreats focus on the meditative practices of mindful eating and living. They involve bringing awareness to all the senses of the eating experience, including attention to the color, texture, smell, and the taste of the food. Another focus is on bringing awareness to hunger cues and recognizing what the body really needs and food portions.

DO I HAVE TO GO ON A RETREAT TO DO MINDFULNESS?

No. As explained in other sections in the book, anything that can be done mindlessly can be done mindfully, and as such, you can be anywhere and doing anything and be mindful. Nevertheless, going on retreat is a great way to immerse yourself into mindfulness and for many serves as a kick start to an enduring mindfulness practice.

IS IT POSSIBLE TO NOT TALK FOR AN ENTIRE WEEKEND?

Yes. In some religious communities and monasteries, for instance, the Trappist Order in Catholicism, practitioners have been silent for many years. The idea of silence is to quiet not just the voice but the mind and body in order to cultivate a calm and peaceful personal and retreat environment. Silence greatly enhances the deepening of focus and awareness. The silence on retreat goes beyond the individual, as it is also a way of not distracting fellow retreatants.

The silence is silence not only of the voice but also of any other forms of communication. Not texting, writing, and signing are recommended in order to stay focused on the task of meditation.

The silence can be broken under the following conditions:

To meet with the teacher: This typically happens in a designated room in order to get guidance about your practice. Perhaps you are sitting in a way that leads to physical pain, or you are experiencing unusual sensations. The teacher can help with putting these into context.

In case of a medical or home emergency: As with anywhere else medical emergencies can occur, or a person has a loved one who is in fragile health and might need to be reached. Usually retreats have point people who will help under these circumstances.

At the end: Silence is broken at the end of the retreat, and this allows people to share their experiences with other retreatants.

ARE THERE BREAKS?

All retreats have lunch, tea, work, and rest breaks during the retreat. These are breaks from the yoga or sitting meditation; however, retreatants are encouraged to take these breaks mindfully: when eating a meal or drinking tea, to do so mindfully; when walking to your room to take a rest, to do that mindfully as well.

WHAT HAPPENS WHEN A MINDFULNESS RETREAT ENDS?

Typically people return to their lives, some transformed by the experience and some not. Some decide to continue to practice what they have learned, while others feel refreshed by the break from everyday life and continue to do what they have always done. One idea that is typically taught at retreats is that there is benefit to continued practice. This makes sense. It would be as if going away to a weight loss or exercise camp and deriving the benefits from having done so but then not continuing when you got home.

If change does occur, it is typically in that people might find you to be quieter, more thoughtful, less judgmental, and less self-involved; however, under typical circumstances, your tastes, choice of friends, sense of humor, and so on don't change in that you and the people who know and love you still recognize you for who you are.

13. What makes for a good mindfulness teacher?

Although it is possible to learn the basics of mindfulness without a teacher, in the long run, having a teacher who can explore experiences and technique is helpful. This is true of almost any of life's endeavors. A skilled teacher can help not only in learning the *how* of mindfulness more quickly but also in learning how to make it more effective.

DO THEY KNOW WHAT THEY'RE DOING?

When learning any complex skill, like learning to play the violin, a new language, and archery, having experienced coaches or guides can make all the difference. The more experienced, the more they will be able to walk the practitioner through the myriad experiences that can come up in a mindfulness practice. Because mindfulness can bring up new internal experiences and observations, they can be hard to decipher, and typically more accomplished guides will have had similar experiences themselves.

DO THEY HAVE THEIR OWN REGULAR PRACTICE?

There is a concept in Zen Buddhism known as *beginner's mind*, and it refers to having an attitude of openness, eagerness, and pure curiosity when participating in any endeavor, and this includes the use of such an attitude even when practicing at an advanced level. In other words, the advanced teacher adopts the same attitude that a beginning learner would. A teacher should be someone who has an enduring practice and who embodies the spirit of a beginner's mind; without such a capacity it is unlikely that the person will be a helpful mentor. Also, because a teacher's practice would lead to present-focused interactions, an effective teacher would tend not to be distracted.

ARE THEY KIND?

One of the benefits of mindfulness practice, although not its specific goal, is that it leads to the development of loving kindness and compassion in the practitioner. For teachers who are mature in their practice, the result should be that they have a spirit of kindness and compassion that visibly flows from themselves to others. That is not to say that they are angelic, are soft-spoken, or live saintly lives, but it is clear to others that they are concerned with the well-being of those around them. If a guru came across as gossipy, mean-spirited, and judgmental, it would be unlikely that the guru would be an effective candidate as a teacher.

DO THEY DEMAND SEX, MONEY, OR POWER?

Mindfulness teachers, like all others, have basic needs, and so it is not wrong for mindfulness teachers to charge for their teaching. A teacher living a luxurious lifestyle in an expensive house and with pricey cars would likely struggle with nonattachment and as such would not be a likely candidate as the type of teacher a student would look for.

There is a concept in Indian philosophy known as *dana* or *daana*, which is the idea of generosity or charity, giving without expecting any form of repayment from the recipient. Mindfulness retreats tend to be inexpensive, and most teachers do not ask for money. Nevertheless, those studying with a teacher will often offer *dana* to help cover some of the living costs. No teacher should ever use their influence and relationship with a student for the purpose of sex, power, or money.

Historically, the relationship between teacher and student was considered sacrosanct, and so sexual affairs were not always condemned. Nevertheless, as in all spiritual and secular disciplines, people in authority, including the mindfulness movement, have abused their power to meet their own ego desires. Often this abuse occurs out of ignorance by the student. For instance, hatha yoga, from which almost all yoga styles evolved, began as a branch of Tantra, which included many sexual practices. The idea was that Tantra devotees sought, through sexual acts, to fuse the male and female nature of humans and the universe into a single and blissful state of consciousness. Teachers who abused this would often instruct that such sexual contact was consistent with the ideal of attaining enlightenment. Students, knowing no better, would often be at the mercy of an unscrupulous teacher. For instance, and he is far from the only one, the famed Zen spiritual leader Eido Shimano who headed a Japanese Buddhist monastery in the Catskills was forced to resign after rumors of sexual affairs with his students and other women came to light, and to which he later confessed. Despite being married, he did not keep to the principle of *right living*.

Another concern would be the abuse of power. Under ordinary circumstances there is a power differential between teacher and student, no less so between a mindfulness teacher and his or her student. A teacher demanding favors, setting up conflict between students, or promising that he or she can deliver special powers would not be the teacher a student should look for.

DO THEY HAVE ENOUGH TIME TO TEACH AND MEET?

Most teachers are not abusive and are devout and disciplined, and yet from a practical perspective, they might not be the right teachers if they do not actually have the time to meet and teach. This would typically happen because the most advanced and virtuous teachers tend to be the ones most in demand and have the least amount of time available for new students. Although the great teachers might not be available, they can often recommend teachers who do have availability. Then, although the most advanced teachers are not available, they are often a part of a larger community and their teaching will often be distilled in group settings.

DOES THE TEACHER NEED TO BE BUDDHIST?

Historically, meditation was not taught as a secular practice but instead within the context of Buddhism, Daoism, and other traditions. The teacher was normally a priest, monk, or guru of that tradition, and the teacher's role was not only to explain the technique but also to teach the principles and ethics of the spiritual tradition with which it was connected. The student would therefor meditate within that tradition. Then and as is true today, in religious and spiritually rooted mindfulness contexts, students would select their teacher based on their character and lineage.

Modern mindfulness practice has brought with it secular meditation, which is tied less to mysticism and more to scientific brain science. This has brought in people of different faiths and those of no faith at all.

The decision as to whether to seek out a spiritual or secular teacher is up to the student. For many people, having a teacher will be a way to kick-start their practice and answer their questions, as well as motivate the person to stay the course. Eventually though it is time to journey on even without the teacher.

There is a well-known teaching that attributed to first-century Zen Master Linji that goes: "If you meet the Buddha, kill him." As with many teachings, it is not literal. The Buddha, road, and the killing are all symbolic. The road is typically interpreted as the path to enlightenment. The Buddha is often considered to be the teacher that has gotten the person started on his or her path. Ultimately, the task is for each person to find his or her own path. Following someone else's path will not get a person to reach his or her own enlightenment, and so "killing" or ultimately discontinuing the path and teachings of another person with the goal of finding one's own way is what is key. A good mindfulness teacher is one who will get a student to become aware of his or her journey and then let the person find his or her own path.

14. Do I need to practice every day, and if so, how long before I see a difference?

A common complaint about mindfulness is that it is too hard to do and that "it doesn't work." Some people feel that trying to "do mindfulness" day after day is a waste of time and does not show enough benefit to be worth the while. Others feel that even if they can be mindful, all they notice is pain and negative thoughts, so why do it?

There are people who practice as few as 10 minutes of mindfulness each day and notice distinct benefit particularly in the form of reduced stress and increased joy. Brains are different, and for some practitioners a small amount of mindfulness practice goes a long way. Typically, research shows that to get enduring benefit, about 20 minutes or more is necessary to notice these benefits.

Many scientific studies bear this out. For people enrolled in mindfulness-based stress reduction (MBSR) research, participants notice the benefits of mindfulness when completing at least 20 minutes of mindfulness every day for eight weeks. This is true even if the research participants were new to meditation. In one study (2011) group participants reported spending an average of 27 minutes meditating. When their brains were scanned and then compared to their brains before the study, the researchers found growth in the part of the brain associated with learning and memory, as well as areas associated with self-awareness, compassion, and attention. These study participants reported a reduction in stress, and this in turn was associated with a decrease in activity in an area of the brain known as the amygdala. The amygdala is most active when a person experiences fear, anxiety, or aggression, as it is responsible for triggering the body's fight or flight response. In this study, none of these beneficial changes were seen in the control group, that is, the comparison group of study participants who were not meditating.

Any amount of meditation is better than none. Many people notice that meditating even just five minutes while sitting can change their experience of the day in a meaningfully positive way. Of course, a person cannot know what would have happened had he or she not meditated; however, the person can recognize typical and habitual patterns of behavior and then see what happens after meditating. The commitment to do some amount every day is key and is similar, for instance, to making the commitment to exercise regularly.

Therefore, if even just five minutes can help and if mindfulness is so beneficial, then why not spend the entire day meditating? Is there a maximum amount of time? Clearly, for most people the time available for meditation is limited. Even on a mindfulness retreat, most people spend only 10 hours of the day meditating. Time is needed to do life's other activities, including sleep. There are monks and nuns who spend decades of their lives meditating, but for the vast majority of us, 20 minutes or so every day can make huge differences.

As with any new learning or new skill, enduring change takes time. For most people, the first sign of progress is an increase in physical relaxation and emotional stability. Even if that appears too subjective, in many cases other people will notice the change because relationships improve in people who meditate, more specifically that the person is friendlier, more relaxed, less reactive, and less moody.

Another sign of progress is an improved ability to concentrate on and pay attention to experiences. With this will often come the recognition that you are more observant and begin to notice details you had not been aware of before. The observations can be of physical objects in our environment, for instance, a flower in the garden or the flavor of a meal, or can be the awareness of a single breath flowing in and out of the lungs.

Some people notice the impact that their posture has on their mind, for instance, how slouching can perpetuate a bad mood and how sitting straight with shoulders back can improve the mood.

Another important sign is the recognition that not every urge needs to be followed: that there is a space between an urge that arises in the mind and the behavior that follows and that in that space there is an opportunity to make a choice. Then, with increasing attention come an awareness of behavior and the consequence of the behavior. You realize not only that you are doing things more deliberately but that you take into account the impact the things you are doing might have.

Ironically, one other sign that you are progressing is, at times, dissatisfaction with the way you are living and the choices that you have made and are making. It can be easy to judge friends who live without such awareness and to judge your behavior and yet in order to change things you first have to become aware of the things you want to be different.

Finally, the most sublime of signs is noticing not getting upset about whether you are making progress or not. It is being at peace with the pace of change, enjoying the good days, and not fretting over the hard days, recognizing that they are just moments on a journey.

15. Can I do other things, like listening to music, while I meditate?

From a historical Buddhist perspective, listening to music while meditating would have been completely disallowed, and there are no Buddhist texts which mention music as part of the practice. In the ancient monasteries, there would have been complete silence or whatever sounds nature provided.

And so an apparent paradox is created by the idea that if a person is sitting in meditation focusing on the moment, it is then not possible for that person to be doing something else, like listening to music, at the same time. This is, however, a narrow view of mindfulness. It is true that if the focus of *sitting* mindfulness is on the breath or some mantra word, then listening or practicing music is not compatible with mindfulness. However, because mindfulness is also a practice of where a person focuses his or her attention, focusing on music is completely compatible with mindfulness. Because of this, inasmuch as a person is focusing on his or her breath, the person cannot then also mindfully listen to music; neither can a person mindfully listening to music then also fully concentrate on the breath.

Here, music is the "other thing" a person could be doing while being mindful. However, much of the following information applies to many other activities, like gardening, bathing, and walking.

There are many different types of music, and listing them all would be beyond the scope of this text; however, for the sake of simplicity, imagine that there is *spiritual music* such as church hymns, chanting, and new age, and then there is nonspiritual music. Given its religious origins, it is natural to think spiritual music is more connected to mindfulness than other types.

One particular form of music specifically tied to meditation is the Gregorian Chant. This is a form of chanting named after Pope Gregory I. The chants were originally performed in monasteries by Catholic monks of the Benedictine order. The chants were considered a form of prayer and meditation. In a 2011 study by researchers at the Advanced Center for Yoga division of the National Institute of Mental Health and Neurosciences in Bangalore, India, brain scans showed that during chanting, there was significant deactivation of the parts of the brain that interfere with mindful focus. In other words, people who were chanting compared to simply making other noises were able to lower the neural activity in the *amygdala*, the part of the brain that generates emotions. The amygdala is also the part of the brain that has a lot of activity in people who have a difficult time meditating.

Therefore, it can appear that research would point to religious chanting as a way to induce meditative states, and certainly if a practitioner finds this form of music to help, it can be a very useful practice. Nevertheless, it is the quality of focus that is important and not the type of music that determines whether mindfulness is present or not.

Part of the confusion, when it comes to mixing music and mindfulness, is that many alternative health practitioners and spas play soothing background music during the treatment appointment, and in many cases this background music has been labeled *meditation music*, music that can be bought at the front desk when the client checks out. Many then make the understandable error in equating spa music with the type of music a person should listen while meditating. The other error is in thinking that because persons may find spa music to be relaxing that when they reach a relaxed state, they are being mindful; however, as we saw in question five, although a benefit of mediation can be a state of relaxation, relaxation is not the purpose of mindfulness, and many people who meditate do not find it to be relaxing. It is important to correct the notion that relaxation and mindfulness are the same thing, and by extension that by listening to relaxing music a person will necessarily reach a mindful state.

In order to listen to music, do gardening, walk, eat, or do any other practice as meditation, it needs to be done one-mindfully. When listening to music as meditation, the task is not to do anything else at the same time. The meditator focuses all attention on the music without also doing homework, reading, or exercising. It can be useful to darken the room in order to reduce visual distractions and more keenly sharpen the sense of hearing. Ideally, the practice is also done while sitting comfortably, rather than lying down which might induce sleepiness.

Although any type of music can be attended to, words of songs carry meaning and can lead to the mind wandering to memories or other associations. Also if the song is familiar and has a catchy tune, a person can be caught up in humming along. Because of this some choose to use recording of natural sounds, such as waves, wind flow, and birdsongs. These natural sounds would have been truer to the Buddha's experience; however, the outdoors is not necessary to practice meditation.

The theme of where a person intentionally places his or her attention will be repeated throughout the book, as this is the essence of mindfulness: all activities like listening to music, gardening, and washing dishes can be meditative practices if done with focused attention on the activity. Similarly, they can all be done mindlessly. Nevertheless, focusing on two things at once is not compatible with the practice of mindfulness.

16. Isn't it better if I use mindfulness time for planning my day and doing things?

There is a joke that goes like this:

Joanne meets her friend on the street and asks: "How's your son doing? Is he still unemployed?"
"Yes," replies the friend, "but he's into sitting mindfulness these days."
"What's that?" asks Joanne.
"I'm not exactly sure but at least it's better than sitting around doing nothing."

A criticism of meditation is that people are simply sitting around contemplating and thinking and that it is a frivolous and self-indulgent waste of time, time that would be better used planning the day and doing things. The paradox is that in this "doing-nothing" the mind heals and then everything is done.

The act of mindfulness is the particular way in which a person pays attention to the task at hand, and that includes every actions and interactions. However, because we are not used to paying attention in this way, sitting quietly in a meditative practice is a powerful way to learn. The criticism that it is "sitting around doing nothing" is a reflection of the observer's point of view. If a person were sitting around watching TV or reading a book, the observer would see that as an action, but the observer of the meditator cannot see the meditator's mind. In the context of a meditative lifestyle, doing nothing other than observing the mind can be considered as a mental surrender, in that it simply notes the urge to do "something" without then acting on the urge. It is tuning in to the present moment and its ever-changing circumstances, recognizing the completeness of the moment without having to do anything about it. In that sense, mindfulness is not a passive state.

In Taoism there is a concept known as wei-wu-wei, which is "the action of nonaction," a core paradox of Taoist teaching. The simplest definition of wei-wu-wei is that it means doing nothing, but more broadly it means not forcing something, allowing events to simply flow without trying to change them. A river flows in the river bed, and when it comes up against a big rock, it continues to flow around the rock without trying to move it. That is the nature of the river, and so the mind flows with thoughts, actions, and urges, and the task is to notice this flow without acting on it. It is in so doing that the practitioner gains the benefits of mindfulness.

In this context, having gained mastery in the skill of observing the mind at work, the practitioner has arguably used his or her time most effectively and efficiently.

The great Yankee baseball player and philosopher Yogi Berra once said about batting: "You can't hit and think at the same time." Elite athletes describe states of effortlessness no-thought also known as being in the "zone," times when they produce their best performances. During these times, there is no thinking; there is simply being in that moment.

The art of doing nothing is the ability to not cling to passing thoughts or emotions but instead move along effortlessly in the current of the mind's flow. If clinging on to a past hurt were the thing that you were doing, then letting go of clinging is the nonaction that leads to freedom from suffering.

During formal sitting mindfulness, also known as *Vipassana*, doing nothing with your thoughts is the technique at the core of the practice. It involves detachment from thoughts, observing them with neither following the thoughts nor pushing them away. The meditator gets to the realization that the conditions for happiness exist in the present moment and as such that there is nothing specific to do. The Zen master Dogen says: "If you cannot find enlightenment right where you are, where else do you expect to find it?" Because of this, there is no searching that needs to take place, only being.

Sitting mindfulness meditation, known as *Vipassana*, is a situation where there is no action other than sitting. The rest of our lives we are always doing things, and in the unrelenting doing we get lost in the never-ending obsessions and thought spirals of our mind. During meditation, by not doing anything all this noise is revealed and then a person has the ability to deal with what actually is rather than what isn't. It is like trying to clean up a room in the dark. By switching on the light, a person sees what needs to be done. Sitting quietly illuminates the mind; in this way the process allows the mind to heal, arguably a very productive effect of doing nothing.

Doing nothing is also a way to connect with all others and life itself because there is no resistance to experiences. This is fundamental to healthy relationships because there is no action in trying to maneuver them one way or another and then disappointment when they don't turn out the way we wanted them to be. There is no agenda to the act of mindfulness other than being open to what is.

IS MINDFULNESS A STATE OF INACTION?

Doing nothing is not a static state of being because everything is in a state of constant change. Thoughts are being thought, the heart is pumping blood, and lungs are breathing air, and so on. However, by recognizing these things as what is happening in the moment, effectiveness blooms. The mindful actress can deliver her lines, the mindful athlete focuses on the target, the mindful gardener considers the condition and nature of the plants and soil, and the mindful therapist listens fully. In all cases the more attuned and attentive the person, the closer he or she gets to his or her goal. The actress wondering if her laundry is done, the athlete considering what to have for supper, the gardener lost in thought about politics, and the therapist thinking about her kids at home are not present with the conditions in front of them; there is a harmony that brings out the best and most effective version of the individual.

17. How do I deal with distractions?

Many people have the experience when paying attention to their mind and body that their minds are very active and bodies very fidgety and that because of this they have a difficult time being mindful. The conclusion is: "If my mind is wandering and I can't sit still, I can't do mindfulness," and yet the fact that a person has noticed a wandering mind and fidgety body is an important first step.

WHY DOES MY MIND WANDER?

In the age of mindfulness, mind-wandering is considered unhealthy, and in many circumstances the wandering mind is considered to be an unhappy mind, one that takes us to dark and unhealthy places. Often this type of experience is the target of mindfulness practice.

The first issue is where the mind wanders off to. Researchers have found that excessive mind-wandering when it is stuck in rumination and worry can have negative effects on health. However, most mind-wandering does not get us into trouble, and in fact, the mind is wired to wander. As the human brain evolved to deal with a constantly changing world, people who were able to consider possible futures, review past mistakes, think about different solutions, and understand how other people's minds work had an evolutionary advantage. The wandering mind is a creative mind, one that sparks innovation and increases productivity by finding ways around time-consuming obstacles, and in many cases such innovations have led to increases in well-being.

Think of the mind as an anthill, with ants as thoughts all going about their business. The brain has many millions of neural connections talking to each other all the time, in order to keep life functioning. Most of the chatter is in the background and is not in our awareness, but, nevertheless, it is essential for survival and jumps to attention when there is a threat or marked change in the routine. When sudden change happens, a lot of brain energy flows to attentional circuits to deal with the situation. Going back to the anthill analogy, imagine that you drop a dab of honey near the anthill. Suddenly all the ants go to the honey; it is novel, a source of instant nutrition, and important to the health of the community. Once all the honey is gone, they scatter back to doing what they were doing.

DO I HAVE TO STOP MY THOUGHTS?

Trying to stop thoughts is like trying to stop the ants from crawling about. The task in mindfulness is less about stopping thoughts than simply observing them. It would be as if pulling up a chair next to the anthill and simply watching the ants crawling about without judging them or trying to control them in any way. The task in mindfulness is simply to observe the comings and goings of thoughts without judgment or trying to change them.

Often, novice meditators will wonder: "Am I doing this right? What is for dinner? I should have sat on a pillow. My back hurts." The more persons sit still with their mind, the more they will be aware of the hundreds of thoughts that arise. Mindfulness is recognizing that they have arisen. Saying "I don't like the thought I am having and so I am going to stop it by thinking about something else" would not be mindfulness.

WHAT IF I LIVE IN A BUSY CITY?

Mindfulness is the practice of noticing what is without reacting. Many people find that going to the country or going away on retreat is the best condition to attain that state of awareness; however, many others don't have the luxury or time of being able to get away from life's demands for any prolonged period of time. The task is to learn to apply the principles of mindfulness in attending to the tasks of everyday life in the regular setting, whether in a green leafy suburb or a chaotic metropolitan center.

Because research shows that it is easier to reach a mindful state in the context of greenery, some people choose to go to their local park or playground to get some semblance of nature. Others choose a room, typically the furthest away from street noise and fill it with potted plants and soft music and use that room as a mini-retreat from the world.

Even if there are no green spaces, or the few that exist are inaccessible due to distance or danger, there are options.

People can use their senses, for instance, the taste of a square of chocolate or a cup of tea, the sound of monks chanting from a video on the Internet, the feel of a piece of fabric, the smell of a flower or coffee beans or incense, and, for sight, the meditation on a pleasant picture or photograph, typically one that is not too emotionally stimulating.

WHY ARE SOME DAYS EASIER THAN OTHERS?

As with any other activity that requires some dedication and effort, mindfulness meditation is no different, in that some days are easier than others. In dealing with coworkers, friends, children, family, and others, some days are easier than others. In exercising regularly, some days are easier than others. In trying to garden or read a book, some days are easier than others. Life is full of distractions and vulnerability factors. The demands of work, the effects of illness and poor sleep, the unexpected event or interaction all influence the ease with which we approach each moment. What is clear over many research studies is that the more mindfulness is practiced, the more accessible it is and the easier it is to do over the long run.

18. Is it okay if I move around while I meditate?

Although many people can sit in one place while watching TV, sitting at a restaurant, sitting at a school desk or in their office cubicle, trying a seated meditation seems almost impossible. Some complain of feeling restless and jittery. Any attempt at meditation leads to aches and pains and squirming. What is a person to do?

There are many reasons that people have for not being able to sit still, especially as beginners to the practice. These include the discomfort of the sensations brought on by paying attention to aches and pains, anxiety and worry thoughts, attention deficit disorder, the recollection of past traumatic experiences, and the belief that it is a waste of time. The solution is fairly simple: rather than a sitting meditation, do something else. For some, this means doing classes like tai chi and yoga, but for others it's as easy as taking a walk.

Historically, meditation was taught to be practiced in different postures depending on context. This was done in order to account for different circumstances; for instance, if the meditator was a monk traveling on a pilgrimage to a distant destination, at any given time he or she would be in one of four common postures: sitting, standing, walking, or lying down. The monk might be sitting during a meal or for a rest, standing while waiting in line, walking on the journey, or lying down to rest or stretch out. The idea is that any of these postures are ones in which mindfulness can be practiced. For people who need to move, a walking meditation can be an effective solution.

As with many things we do as humans, once a behavior becomes habitual, it loses its novelty. A child delights in being able to get up and walk, a child when it first gets up on a bicycle without training wheels, and a teen when he or she first learns to drive. And yet as the person ages, none of these activities and skills seems that impressive, and they are taken for granted.

In sitting meditations, the practitioner typically initially anchors his or her attention on the breath. In walking meditation, the attention is focused on the act of walking, and there are various ways to do this. Before beginning, the person stands still for a moment and becomes aware of his or her body in space. The person feels the feet in his or her shoes, the shoes on the ground, and the ground supporting the person's weight. Next is a focus on all the small and subtle movements necessary in keeping a person upright and balanced. The key task here is simply being aware of standing and all that goes into it.

Then the person takes the first step and shifts his or her attention from standing to the physical sensation of walking. This means feeling the soles of the feet as the person makes contact with the walking surface and then the absence of sensation when the foot is lifted.

Another way to walk mindfully is to pay careful attention to the combination of physical movements, for example, thinking "left" when the left foot is lifted; noting the muscles of the thigh, the bend of the knee, the angle of the ankle, and then the strike of the foot. Next comes noticing shifting the weight forward and repeating the practice on the right foot. The stepping is slow and meticulous, with each action carefully attended to.

Some choose to do the walking meditation out in nature; however, a large open space is not necessary. It can take place in a small office or bedroom. In small spaces, it involves taking a few steps forward, turning around slowly, and then walking back the other way.

The walking meditation can be done at any pace, from a normal walking speed to extremely slow. Some people find that slower pace allows for more attention on all aspects of the meditative walk, including beyond the leg motion: the movement of the arms, the flow of the breath, and stability of core muscles.

Setting aside the mindfulness benefits of walking in nature, there are also health benefits when comparing walking in nature to walking in city environments. In two recent Japanese research (2015), people who fully experienced the sights, sounds, and smells of the forest had lower concentrations of cortisol in their blood, lower pulse rate, and lower blood pressure after the exposure to nature than when they first started the study.

Even if mindfulness is difficult while walking, there are other benefits of taking a walk, particularly in nature. The increase in activity leads to fresh air flowing into the lungs and then in turn increased blood flow to the muscles and the brain and, with that, a burst of creativity. For many artists and writers, meandering through nature or a city park as a daily practice is a way to clear the mind and experience creativity.

19. What if I am the only one of my friends practicing?

Many people who start to practice mindfulness will have the experience of having their close friends wondering what they are up to. In many cases, a person who finds mindfulness to be a useful addition to his or her daily routine also finds that the practice is met with skepticism and curiosity from close friends and family. This makes sense, and the response is not that different than if one in a group of friends suddenly decided to start running marathons or became a wine aficionado or any other departure from the predictable daily flow of behaviors, particularly when none of the others in the group has ever expressed any interest or desire in that activity.

One of the paradoxes about mindfulness—paradoxes are common in Buddhist teachings—is that although it is a practice that has been shown to bring people together and enhance relationships through embracing the moment and accepting people in their fragility and completeness exactly as they are, it is also a practice that can leave the practitioner feeling isolated. Imagine that you are sitting on a bus surrounded by people. Rather than burying your head in your smartphone or newspaper, you sit mindfully engaged and wishing loving compassion toward all. You look around and see that your fellow travelers are lost in their music, texting, or reading, and you see how disconnected you are from the others. The very awareness that you need to connect to others is the same awareness that lets us see just how disconnected we can be from each other under many circumstances.

Another concern stems from a curious need that most of us have, and that is this: people who embark on journeys of self-exploration and discovery tend to want to spend a lot of time talking about it. However, it is often clear that others don't necessarily want to hear. Because the meditator can be so caught up in the fascination of his or her experience, he or she wants all to know, and yet it is typical that only others who have been there can appreciate it or are tolerant to listening for more than one telling. Like the marathon runner going on and on with a group of friends about running 26 miles, there comes a point when it is too much and the discussion can then be alienating. Inasmuch as the experience can be exhilarating for the individual, for all the inner peace, grounding, reduced anxiety, and self-acceptance it provides, the experience when shared can be boring and seen as a rude intrusion by others.

Mindfulness is awareness, and it includes the awareness that others might not be interested. It also means accepting things as they are in the present moment. This includes the fact that friends and family might not be receptive to the idea of mindfulness. If those close to the practitioner come across as dismissive, argumentative, or condescending, it can be tough to practice compassion and to remember that others too are human beings on their own journey with their own aspirations.

One approach to integrating others is articulated in Buddhism's Eightfold Path, the formula for how to live, and it includes having the right attitude by not harboring thoughts of greed and anger toward others. Next is using the right speech, which means to avoid lying, gossip, and mean-spirited speech. Other aspects of the Eightfold Path include avoiding occupations and actions that bring harm to others and, then by using the power of mindfulness, to love and to see people and things in their true nature, products of their causes and consequences.

By using skillful communication and compassion, relationships will improve, or at least not worsen, as open acceptance and communication is central to maintaining healthy interconnectedness.

The meditator may find that his or her friends and family find the mindfulness practice to be more than just an oddity and experience non-acceptance and disapproval. Sometimes it is because others feel that mindfulness practice clashes with their culture or religion, and at other times it is because of specific choices. For instance, some practitioners are vegetarian, and they come to this choice noting that the business enterprises which produce meat products also create fear and suffering for a large number of animals which are penned into massive industrial enclosures and force fed for the sole purpose of getting large quantities of meat to market. Although eating meat is not prohibited in Buddhism, there is a mindfulness contemplation that focuses on the suffering and death of nonhuman, and how this suffering and death contributes to human comfort. For some, this contemplation leads to be less inclined to consume simply out of comfort.

Another place where close kin might take issue is in the use of alcohol. Some meditators abstain from alcohol because of its effects on the mind. Abstaining can take its toll on relationships, particularly during holiday festivities and social gatherings. Drinking alcohol can be a problem when it changes from being a pleasant experience to a way to escape the challenges of the present moment or the demons of past experiences. Then sometimes when a person drinks too much and lashes out at loved ones, it further impacts relationships. Excessive drinking, like the effects of other excesses, can dramatically and adversely impact the brain's capacity to attend and focus.

A mindfulness practitioner choosing a vegetarian or alcohol-abstinent lifestyle is an example of when he or she may experience the judgment of those around. Although the support of family and friends is welcome when a person chooses a life of contemplation, such support is not essential. Actively seeking approval, particularly from disapproving family members and friends, can lead to isolation and resentment. Life and relationships will change, but that is true in any cases. The nature of life is enduring change. For the practitioner, the task is to practice as a way to enhance the wondrous experience of each moment, including relationships. In so doing, even if the journey leads the person through moments of distancing from others, in the long run, the benefits to relationships far outweigh any temporary distancing that may occur.

20. How do drugs and alcohol impact mindfulness?

Mindfulness is about awareness in the present circumstance. Circumstances are not always ideal, and meditators have meditated while hungry, cold, and sleep deprived. These conditions lead to different states of mind, and this in turn changes the brain's ability to focus. Environmental factors change the brain, and it is constantly changing because of learning, aging, responding to illness, and so on. The effect of drugs and other substances whether legal, illegal, or prescribed, and including alcohol, caffeine, and nicotine, also impacts how the brain perceives reality.

ALCOHOL

Traditional monastic meditative life is different from Western reality. The consumption of all forms of intoxicants is commonplace, and although there are benefits, the effects can readily lead to confusion, impulsivity, and recklessness, as many an ill-considered, post-partying text message and e-mail has proven. Accepting that historical accounts of the Buddha are accurate, we know then that he drank alcohol in his youth. Over time, he recognized that the use of alcohol put him on a slippery slope to loss of control, and so in abstinence he taught that alcohol was a poison that clouded the inherent clarity of the mind.

Although alcohol was initially forbidden, as Buddhism spread and encountered different cultures, it adapted to them, and today in many monastic settings in Tibet and India, alcohol is accepted. For instance, a branch of Buddhism known as Vajrayana or "Tibetan Buddhism" includes alcohol in its practice. The idea is that once a meditator has established meditative discipline and incorporated it in his or her life, he or she then takes on previous prohibitions. In Vajrayana it takes several years to get to this point. Alcohol is seen as a potential aide for the meditator as a tool for loosening the ego's clinging to perceived reality. When this practice was brought to the West, the guru Chogyam Trungpa Rinpoche referred to it as "mindful drinking." In the United States trials of the practice brought mixed results, in that some of his students found that it met the goal of dissolving the delusion of separateness, whereas others became nauseated to the point of throwing up.

Outside of mindful drinking, multiple experiences show that as the amount of alcohol imbibed increases, the capacity for mindfulness decreases. If one were to drink mindfully, it would be a small quantity of a preferred beverage. In this case the person would take his or her favorite wine, beer, or hard alcohol and do the following:

- Mindfully taste it. This is done much in the same way as mindfully drinking a cup of coffee or mindfully eating a bite of food. The task is not to gulp it down but to smell it first, slowly bringing awareness to the taste and the feel on the palate. A large quantity is not necessary.
- Mindfully notice the effects. The meditator then notices what happens to his or her mind's activity as he or she drinks. The meditator notices the effects of the alcohol with each sip, including the loosening of inhibitions. It is important not to judge the effects.
- Find the limit. There is a point at which the mind slips from relaxed openness into drunken silliness and beyond. The task here is to know oneself and stop at the point before going over that edge.
- Evaluate. If the experience was helpful and enhanced the mindfulness practice, the person can consider repeating. If not, continuing to drink is not necessary.

In a 2009 article written by NPR commentator Ted Rose entitled "Mindful Drinking," he asked spiritual teacher Bill McKeever how to know when you've reached the limit. McKeever replies: "Imagine you are enjoying a picnic in a beautiful spot with your lover. You want for nothing in this situation." The point is that similar to the practice of mindfulness, there is no reason to drink to the point of excess. The meditator does not want to lose the delight of the moment. The meditator drinks just enough to be in a relaxed state, to appreciate it and to be fully present in it.

HALLUCINOGENS

In 1943, the Swiss chemist Dr. Albert Hofmann discovered hallucinogenic drug lysergic acid diethylamide (LSD). In the 1960s, and as it is known today, it was called "acid" and became a popular street drug because of its ability to change states of consciousness. In 1966 it was criminalized by the U.S. Congress due to its alleged harmful effects; nevertheless, it is the most researched of all the hallucinogenic or psychedelic drugs and is making a comeback as a possible substance for treating certain psychiatric disorders.

In 1992 psychiatrist Stan Grof, MD, a researcher in non-ordinary states of consciousness including mindfulness, studied its effects and wrote that LSD could be "to psychology what the microscope is to biology" and that "with deep introspection we can view our thoughts coalesce."

Although there is plentiful research on the multiple effects of the drugs, there are almost no studies on its effects on mindfulness. There are anecdotal accounts of Buddhist monks considering its use as a short-cut to supposed enlightenment. This is because LSD has many effects, including the dissolution of self-boundaries, psychotic, ecstatic, and meditative states, and people who have experienced the enlightened awareness state of mindfulness as well as the use of LSD claim that there are similarities between the two states. One problem with considering LSD as a route to enlightenment is that for many who take LSD, it comes at a cost. Like for other drugs, the ensuing mental states fade quicker with each use, and many people require increasing quantities of the drug in order to attain the feeling of connectedness they seek. The increase in consumption is often then accompanied with side effects such as flashbacks, bad trips, and the risk of a bad batch of drug with significant contaminants.

Dr. Roland Fischer is an experimental psychiatrist who explored states of mind in the context of people with schizophrenia, a psychiatric condition where a person hears voices and sees things that are not tangibly there. He wondered if the experiences of a person with schizophrenia were similar to those of people taking hallucinogenic drugs and came up with a model for altered states of consciousness. He categorized these states on what he termed the "perception-hallucination continuum" (1971). On one end of the continuum, he described high-energy chaotic states, such as the mental states in schizophrenia, and, on the other end, restful meditative states such as those experienced during deep meditation. His research found that using low to moderate doses of drugs like LSD could lead to the type of tranquility found in meditation; however, this was not guaranteed, and some experienced the chaotic, unwanted high-energy states on the other end of the continuum.

Then, other than leading to hallucinations and dissolution of boundaries, the hallucinogens like LSD could cause a remarkable distortion of time ranging from (typically) an overestimation of time, with time seeming to drag on, to a marked contraction of time where time appears to fly by. The most famous example of this happened on Monday, April 19, 1943, a day that was to become known as "Bicycle Day." Hofmann took LSD just before embarking on his typical two-and-a-half mile cycle ride home. He detailed the experience in his 1979 autobiography. "I had to struggle to speak intelligibly. I asked my laboratory assistant to escort me home. On the way, my condition began to assume threatening forms. Everything in my field of vision wavered and was distorted as if seen in a curved mirror. I also had the sensation of being unable to move from the spot. Nevertheless, my assistant later told me that we had travelled very rapidly."

PRESCRIPTION DRUGS

Prescription drugs, meaning medications prescribed by physicians (tranquilizers, antianxiety drugs, antidepressants, muscle relaxants, etc.), also change the experience of the mind. For the meditator there are pros and cons; on the one hand, they can put people into states where they are better able to tolerate discomfort and therefore be capable of sitting in meditation, yet on the other hand, they can also dull cognitive processes, which can have side effects involving the liver and other organs.

Whether or not drugs and alcohol have a helpful role in mindfulness is questionable. Certainly, they have many side effects and can rapidly and significantly impact a person's health, and in some cases they can be so habit-forming and expensive that they leave the user financially and relationally impoverished.

◆❖◆

The Historical Origins
of Mindfulness

21. Is mindfulness a religion?

Mindfulness is not a religion. It is the practice of compassionate, nonjudgmental, and intentional awareness of the present moment. This includes
all of the things the present moment contains, including not just the
external world but also thoughts, physical sensations, and emotions.

It can be easy to see why many think that it is a religion. The word
"mindfulness" itself often conjures up images of Buddhist monks meditating on hilltops. It is certainly a core practice of Buddhist life; however,
so are eating, sleeping, and walking, and yet we do not consider eating,
sleeping, and walking to be particularly Buddhist.

A typical definition of religion includes the idea of a system of beliefs
and doctrine that conceptualizes an ultimate reality or deity. Further, it
also typically has a code of ethical conduct, and then finally there are rituals, observances, places of worship, and devotions that identify specific
religious practices. Spiritual practices within specific faith require that its
practice be followed in certain defined ways, articulated in the religious
texts of the faith, in order for an individual to be considered as a member
of the particular religion.

Mindfulness requires none of this. Although there are many books
written on mindfulness, there is no bible. There are books written on
running and cooking, but these are not religious in nature, and there is no

need for faith or mysticism in order to run or cook even though for some people running and cooking can be spiritual experiences. Mindfulness has not set rituals, no places of worship, no days dedicated to observance, and no code of ethics to follow.

IF IT'S NOT A RELIGION, IS THERE A CONNECTION TO RELIGION?

In the next few questions, the connection to religion will be more fully examined. Mindfulness is the way a person attends to being in the world. Although it has its origins in the contemplative practices of ancient religions like Buddhism, Hinduism, and Taoism, and even though many of today's religions have meditative practices, in and of itself, it is no religion, in that mindfulness has no deity associated with it. People of many faiths share common practices, like congregating, singing, and taking care of the needy, but none of these practices are a religion. In a secular context, people congregate at bars and sporting events, sing in their glee clubs, and help the needy from a humanistic perspective or out of self-indulgent pleasure.

To underscore this point, many secular philosophies have incorporated the value of such awareness. For instance, the Roman philosopher Epictetus, born a slave, shared the following wisdom 2,000 years ago:

Man is not worried by real problems so much as by his imagined anxieties about real problems,

which speaks to the insight that it is the working of the mind not focused on the present moment reality but what the mind does with it that is problematic. Here is another quote:

Demand not that things happen as you wish, but wish them to happen as they do, and you will go on well.

Here the focus is on accepting that things are the way they are.

Emperor Marcus Aurelius, who ruled Rome a century after Epictetus, was similarly a Stoic and shared his perspective on the mindful life: "You have power over your mind—not outside events. Realize this, and you will find strength." This speaks to the power of observing how a person observes the functioning of his or her mind; then "the happiness of your life depends upon the quality of your thoughts" is a testament to deciding how to interpret life's events and the choices we make, and finally, "our life is what our thoughts make it" again focuses on the realization that we are masters of our mind if we pay attention to it.

These perspectives on the quality of thought did not come from a religious dictate, and similarly the idea of compassion and love, whereas it abounds throughout all religious writings, belongs to none of them, and many nonreligious people are capable of loving and being compassionate.

Many of our traditions whether religious, secular, or philosophical have aspects of mindfulness in common. These include the focus on love and compassion and the practice of focusing attention on one thing, whether it is on God, the breath, or the hunting down of an animal. In all aspects of human life, throughout its evolution the ability to bring attention to particular endeavors has been associated with survival, and although we cannot know the degree to which such focus was an intentional practice or not, it is an ability that has transcended time, ritual, and religion.

22. Is mindfulness practice compatible with different religions?

There are two questions that frequently come up when people are thinking about practicing mindfulness. The first one commonly comes up in clinics where mindfulness is a component of the treatment, therapies like dialectical behavior therapy (DBT) and mindfulness-based stress reduction (MBSR). The question is, Given that mindfulness has Buddhist roots, will meditation practice interfere with my commitment to my Christian/Jewish/Muslim faith? The second question is, I practice mindfulness within my faith. Do I have to change what I am doing? Or, alternatively, is there a way to practice using my faith? The answer is that all religions have meditative practices within them, and a person does not have to be religious to practice mindfulness. It is also the case that a person who is deeply religious can practice mindfulness in a spiritual way or in a secular fashion. Here is how each religion incorporates mindfulness into its faith.

HOW DO BUDDHISTS PRACTICE?

In Buddhism, meditation focuses simply on body and the mind, and ultimately seeing the mind and body as a single entity. The idea is that everything is one and that we are deluded into believing that we are separate from other things. There is a concept within their practice known as *advaita*, or nonduality. Nondual means "not two, but one." In Buddhism this oneness is the fundamental quality of everything and that everything is a part of and made of one nondual consciousness. For many who struggle with this, the question arises, "If everything is one, why don't I experience it that way?"

This is confusing oneness for sameness, which means that things can appear different without being separate. For instance, the human body has many different body parts but is one thing. All come together to be one body. Similarly, people, animals, plants, rivers, and mountains all have different appearances and ways of being, and yet all come from the same source.

Astronauts recognize this when they get far from earth and see the tininess of our planet. When we drill down on everything in the universe, the building block of each entity is identical. And so, even though there are infinite ways in which objects and experiences can be expressed, they all remain as part of one.

• In Buddhism, the meditator is not focusing on a spiritual entity or deity. The focus is on becoming aware on nonduality. To this end, Buddhist meditative practice can be as an individual or in a group. When meditating in a group—for instance, during a retreat which is also known as a *sesshin* or in a meditation room or *zendo*—the meditator has the benefit of being reminded that he or she is part of a larger Buddhist community, a part of a larger community of people including non-Buddhists, and a part of the community of beings that are not human and then the world, the solar system, galaxy, and universe.

HOW DO CHRISTIANS PRACTICE?

Different from the Eastern traditions of meditation which focus on the goal of transcending the mind and attaining enlightenment, mystical and meditative practices in Christianity focus on the contemplative practice with the goal of moral purification and deeper understanding of the Bible in turn leading to a closer connection to God. Unlike Eastern meditation techniques which do not require any belief, Christian contemplative practices presuppose a belief in Christ and are guided by the teachings of the Bible. There are three main practices:

1. Contemplative prayer: Before Eastern meditative practices were better known in the West, the word "meditation" was synonymous with "contemplation," and people in a state of contemplative prayer were known as meditators. Contemplative prayer practice has two

main streams. The first is known as *centering prayer*—most commonly associated with the practice of Trappist monks, a Catholic order. The second is known as *Christian Meditation*, developed but the Irish Benedictine monk John Main, who had learned mantra meditation from a Hindu teacher when Main was serving in Malaysia.

Here's an example: The meditator chooses a sacred word or name from the Bible, such as "Lord," "Father," "Jesus," "Love," or "Faith." For the next 10–30 minutes the sacred word is repeated with pure focus on the word and without drifting into mechanical repetition. When thoughts or emotions arise, the meditator brings his or her mind back to the sacred word.

2. Contemplative reading: This would not be considered a meditation in Eastern practice because it includes the act of active thinking, deepening understanding and contemplation about the teachings and events in the Bible. An example of this would be choosing a short passage from the Bible and then memorizing it and repeating it silently for some time. All ideas, thoughts, and images that arise during the practice are attended to. The meditator uses reasoning, thinking, and imagination to increase and heighten the personal relationship with God. This is much more active than Eastern practices, in that as the person visualizes, for example, scenes from the life of Christ or the saints, the goal is to live a more engaged and saintly life.

An advanced and more directed practice was developed by the Christian saint, Ignatius of Loyola. It is a practice that takes four weeks to complete and involves the guidance of a spiritual adviser and includes the use of imagery where the meditator enters a biblical scene. The first week involves contemplation on the purpose of one's life and the relationship with God. In the next week the contemplation is on the consequences of sin. In the third week the meditator focuses on the life and death of Jesus. The final week is devoted to experiencing the joy of Christ's resurrection and the recognition of God's love.

3. Sitting with God: This is a silent meditation which follows contemplative prayer or reading and involves the focus of mind, heart, and soul on the presence of God. There is no thinking or contemplation but rather the deep sense of surrendering completely to God and being one with God and the love of God. This is most similar to the focused attention of Eastern meditation where everything else is cast aside and the only focus is on God.

HOW DO JEWS PRACTICE?

Within Judaism there is the ancient practice of Kabbalah, which, broadly, is wisdom derived from the mystical interpretation of the Bible. Literally, the word "Kabbalah" means "to receive" and focuses on the fulfillment of an individual's life. Kabbalah is divided into three categories:

> The spiritual or theoretical: This is the dominant contemporary form of studied and practiced Kabbalah. The goal is to reach higher states of consciousness through meditation on external dimensions by focusing on the divine and the spiritual realm. Theoretical Kabbalah provides landmarks to determine a person's spiritual place in the world, for instance, whether the person is on the side of good or of evil.
>
> The practical or magical: This is the highest form of Kabbalah and was considered the most dangerous, in that it involved the use of supernatural powers, derived from the almighty, to alter and influence the course of nature. It uses the name of God, magic spells and seals, and various other mystical exercises in order to influence the course of events.
>
> The meditative: This focuses on uniting the meditator with God through meditation on the name of God. Similar to Christian contemplative reading, *Kabbalists*, those who practice Kabbalah, use the reading of biblical passages as meditation. Meditative Kabbalah exists in the space between the theoretical and the practical.

The goals of meditative Kabbalah include the heightening of the understanding of the Torah and religious observances, the increase in awareness of the needs of others, the promotion of greater closeness to God, and the disciplining of the mind bringing into awareness aspects of experiences that had previously been unconscious.

Here is an example: Kabbalists view the Hebrew letters as the agents of creation. There are many techniques for visualizing and working with the letters. Jewish lore, known as the *Sefer Yetsirah*, teaches that God created the letters and formed them with all of creation and all that will be created. The meditator visualizes the process of creation of the letters.

The meditator starts by closing or half-closing his or her eyes. The meditator projects images as if on a screen on the back of his or her eyelids. Next the person *engraves* or outlines the letter onto the screen mind's eye with the intent to then work with the specific letter. Then there is the process of *carving*, which entails focusing on the letter as a powerful presence in the consciousness. The task is to focus energy in such a way that the letter is imagined as blazing with fire in the projection. Next is the task of *weighing*, where the meditator is receptive to the qualities of the letter, its meaning, its parts, and its relationship to other letters. The letters are *permuted*, meaning that they are connected with other letters as they arise in the mind, and the task is to focus on the relationship with the combination of letters. Finally, the meditator focuses on the meaning of the combinations, whether they belong together and, if so, the qualities and experience of the created word, for instance, is there harmony or tension between the letters? The belief is that in this practice the focus on God's creation, the Hebrew letters, gets the meditator closer to God and the mind of God.

HOW DO MUSLIMS PRACTICE?

Sufism is the mystical realm of Islam. It is a tradition of meditation, introspection, and prayer that has been practiced since the 12th century and is captured in the writings of the great Sufi poet Rumi, for instance:

> *The drum of the realization of the promise is beating,*
> *we are sweeping the road to the sky. Your joy is here today,*
> *what remains for tomorrow?*
> (Rumi, *The Masnavi*, ca. 1273)

The theme of here and now is clear within this couplet.

The main goal of Sufism is to free people from the "illusory experience" of life in order to allow them to connect to the divine. Common meditative practices include spinning in time with music, intentionally facing pain and sorrow, and opening themselves to new experiences in order to recognize and then challenge habitual behaviors in order to transcend beyond the material world and attain connection with God. In Sufism, there is the concept of the "illusory self," driven by physical desires and suffering and focused on the self, a concept akin to the Western concept of ego. The idea within Sufi meditation is that by taking part in rituals such as the practice of focusing on the divine, the illusory self—which is considered the source of suffering—will be freed.

HOW DO HINDUS PRACTICE?

Hinduism is considered to be the world's oldest religion and has meditative practices woven throughout. There are essentially two forms of Hindu meditative practices, Vedic and yogic.

Vedic meditation: This was developed nearly 5,000 years ago in India as a way for nonreligious people, "ordinary people" to experience

the benefits of mindfulness. Some people know it as "OM" meditation because the practitioner starts by sitting comfortably with eyes
closed and accessing deeper levels of consciousness through the use
of a meaningless sound known as a *mantra*. The idea is not to focus
or concentrate or think but simply chant the mantra and that this
leads to deep states of awareness.

Yogic meditation: This is a more spiritual/religious meditative path
that is integrated with yoga, which is reviewed earlier in question 5.
As previously described, there are eight steps to be worked through
in order to reach ultimate union and awareness. The final three of
these steps are collectively known as *samyama*, with step six being
the practice of *dharana*, step seven being *dhyana*, and step eight
samadhi.

Dharana is the focusing of attention on a single object and the disen-
gagement from other distractions. Once the focus has been established on
the object, *dhyana* is the immersion of the self in the total experience of
uninterrupted connection. *Samadhi* is the state that occurs when only the
essence of the object fills the mind, and the experience is as if the object
were formless. The experience is not clouded by thought, emotions, or
sensations.

HOW DO ATHEISTS PRACTICE?

Outside of religion, all mindfulness practices are secular. People who
describe themselves as atheists will sometimes experience an altered state
of consciousness during meditation, a state that leaves them experiencing awe. When this happens, the experience is often described in spiritual, though nonreligious, terms. Even when this happens, the practice
of mindfulness in a nonreligious/secular context is that which has been
addressed throughout the book and that is the building of focused awareness, and that starts with the commitment to intentionally attend to the
breath and the body's sensations.

23. When did mindfulness come to the United States?

Although there were individuals or small groups who practiced meditation as part of their religion or as an individual activity, Eastern mindfulness did not have much of a presence in the United States until the
late 1960s. In the 1960s the Zen Buddhist movement began to establish

centers throughout the country. It is not uncommon for alternative ideas to take root in the West Coast and, in particular, California, and mindfulness meditation is no exception.

As awareness of meditation increased in the United States, initially U.S. travelers had headed to India and Thailand for formal insight meditation, more properly known as *Vipassana*. For instance, American Buddhist Joseph Goldstein, a graduate of Columbia University, went to Thailand with the Peace Corps in 1962 and later studied *Vipassana* in India. American Buddhist monk Jack Kornfield similarly joined the Peace Corps and studied in Thailand. In 1976, he together with Goldstein and Sharon Salzberg bought a monastic house in rural Barre, Massachusetts, and created the first major Buddhist retreat center in America, the Insight Meditation Society (IMS). Later In 1985 Kornfield and others established IMS West, also known as the Spirit Rock Center in Marin County, California. By the end of the 1980s, these American-born and American-trained students of Eastern Buddhists were accepted as Buddhist teachers tied to the ancient Asian lineages. It was the first time that Americans were accepted into these lineages, and these teachers have in turn taught other American-born students and subsequent teachers.

Although the early pioneers of the American meditation movement had traveled East to study, Eastern Buddhists were coming to the United States at the same time and setting roots in America. The San Francisco Zen Center was established in 1961, and this was followed by the Zen Center in Los Angeles in 1966. The East Coast followed quickly, with Buddhists establishing the Rochester Zen Center in 1966, the New York Zen Studies Society in 1968 ping-ponging back to California with the Shasta Abbey in 1970, and then others. However, despite their presence, many commentators believe that the key moment in awakening America to meditation was in 1968. *The Beatles*, the famed British rock band, traveled to India, to attend a meditation retreat at the ashram of Maharishi Mahesh Yogi, a guru they had met in Wales. Because of their universal fame, their retreat brought widespread awareness of the practice meditation.

One of the first popular books on the subject *Be Here Now* was published in 1971 by former Harvard psychologist Ram Dass. Harvard cardiologist Dr. Herbert Benson followed up by conducting revolutionary studies using meditation to treat heart disease. After Benson published pioneering research, the number of studies looking at the effects of meditation increased dramatically.

In 1979, psychologist Dr. Jon Kabat-Zinn developed mindfulness-based stress reduction (MBSR) at the University of Massachusetts Medical

School. MBSR was developed for patients for whom all else had failed and was focused on targeting severe chronic pain or anxiety in people with various illnesses (MBSR is reviewed more completely in other questions). His program was so successful that the medical school opened a Center for Mindfulness in 1995.

At about the same time that Kabat-Zinn was developing MBSR, psychologist Dr. Steven Hayes at the University of Nevada designed acceptance and commitment therapy (ACT), which is also a mindfulness-based therapeutic technique. ACT was less focused on formal meditation and more on looking at the relationship between thought and behavior. The task in ACT is to recognize thoughts are simply thoughts and do not have to be followed by specific behavior.

Dr. Marsha Linehan at the University of Washington further showed the utility of mindfulness when she adapted the technique to treat patients with borderline personality disorder (BPD). She developed dialectical behavior therapy (DBT) in the early 1990s as a way to target suicidal and self-injurious behavior in women with BPD. DBT integrated Eastern Zen Buddhist mindfulness with Western cognitive behavioral change strategies and became a highly effective treatment for self-destructive behaviors.

In the West there appear to have been major reasons that people sought out mindfulness meditation. One is a psychological and medical treatment for all forms of maladies, treatments such as those just described. The second is a nonreligious spiritual practice for those dissatisfied with either their current religious practice or the nonreligious seeking a deeper meaning. These two uses of mindfulness divergent from their original context within Buddhist practice have meant bringing adaptations to allow if to flourish in the West.

Today, books on mindfulness and meditation are commonplace in American bookstores. Mainstream magazines devote entire editions to meditation, and Zen has become synonymous with everything "new age," and many products attach the term "Zen" as a way of implying wholesome, healthy, spiritual, and green. Certainly Buddhists would never have imagined their spiritual practice to be connected with snack bars and facial creams, and yet because of the association of Zen with simplicity, relaxation, peace, and harmony, marketers clearly intend to connect their product with these values.

In the United States on the one end of Zen practice, there are those who stick to the foundational meditative rituals consistent with the original interpretations. However, even in adherent settings, there have been adaptations. For instance, in many retreats there are chairs for meditators to sit on, a comfort not typical in the East. In the West, dealing with self-hatred, greed, and self-judgment are commonplace but foreign concepts within Tibetan Buddhism and as such were hard to address using traditional Eastern practices. It was in particular because of the amount of self-loathing that loving-kindness meditation became a particularly American focus.

On the other end of the continuum is less meditation and mindfulness as part of a religious experience and more a secular spirituality. It is not unusual to find predominantly white, older, and middle- to upper-middle-class people attending retreats. This is often born out of a longing for fulfillment and satisfaction, a wanting for something more. The irony is not lost on traditional Buddhists that people who appear to have everything they want are still in such desperate need.

Another adaptation has been the use of mindfulness within specific domains of culture such as sports, business, and academics. In these contexts, mindfulness is much more narrowly focused on the outcome and as such much more goal focused. This is in contrast with Eastern practice, which has the typically paradoxical goal in mindfulness of having no-goal.

24. Are there famous people who practice mindfulness?

People have meditated for thousands of years, and in that time, some practitioners became universally known. Throughout the centuries famous and not famous people have meditated. It can sometimes seem that meditation is a thing of the past; however, people considered famous today, in many cases role models for the current generation, are meditators.

A recurring theme in religious transformation and awakening in the best-known spiritual leaders is that of enlightenment, the moment when they realize the truth. For instance, consider the following people.

Jesus: In the New Testament book Matthew, chapter 4, verse 10, there is a description of Jesus going into the desert to meditate on God to fast for 40 days. There he encounters the devil, who tempts him with the promise of food, power, wealth, and desire if he will only give up his quest. Jesus turns him away realizing the truth and the nature of desire getting in the way of realizing the truth.

Jesus appears to have consolidated this wisdom into teachable points; for example, in the book of Luke, chapter 17, verse 21, Jesus had been tending to the sick when he was asked by the congregation the question of when the kingdom of heaven would come. He answered that they should not look to the outside for the kingdom: "Neither 'Look, here.' or, 'Look, there.' for the Kingdom of God is within you." Consistent with contemporary mindfulness meditation, Jesus taught his followers to recognize that heaven lay within them and that they did not need to look outside by seeking here or there.

Mohammed: The Islamic prophet Mohammed spent much of his time meditating before receiving his revelation from the Angel Gabriel as a message from God. Once received, the revelations became the foundation of the Muslim holy text, the Quran. His meditations took place in a cave in a mountain, which subsequently became known as "Jabal-al-Nour" or the Mountain of Enlightenment.

George Fox: George Fox, the founder of Quakerism, was dissatisfied with the hypocrisy of the Christianity of his time. He saw little compassion coming from preachers who spoke of compassion at the pulpit but then turned their backs on those suffering. He meditated on this and realized he needed to break away. After deep contemplation and meditation, he writes in his autobiography: "Now I was come up in spirit through the flaming sword, into the paradise of God. All things were new; and all the creation gave unto me another smell than before, beyond what words can utter. I knew nothing but pureness, and innocency, and righteousness; being renewed into the image of God by Christ Jesus, to the state of Adam, which he was in before he fell. The creation was opened to me; and it was showed me how all things had their names given them according to their nature and virtue."

Isaiah: The biblical prophet Isaiah is the first-considered mystic within the Kabbalistic Jewish tradition. In the Bible he has a vision which scholars consider to be his moment of enlightenment when God (Isaiah 6:9–10) tells him that only the righteous people will see him. As for the rest, God tells Isaiah to tell his people:

> Be ever hearing, but never understanding; be ever seeing, but never perceiving. Make the heart of this people calloused; make their ears dull and close their eyes. Otherwise they might see with their eyes, hear with their ears, understand with their hearts, and turn and be healed.

Here again, writing from nearly 3,000 years ago speaks to the relevance of awareness in reaching spiritual union with God.

Buddha: The best-known story of enlightenment is that of the Buddha. There are countless accounts of the moment told by many authors, but essentially the story goes that in his search for the truth, on a full-moon day in May, he sat in deep meditation under the Bodhi tree. He said that he would not leave the spot until he had found the way to an end of human suffering. He sat there for three days and similarly to the experience of Jesus he was visited by the evil one, who in Buddhist religion is known as Mara. Similarly, the evil one tried to tempt him away from his virtuous path by offering beautiful women and pleasure, and then when that did not work, lightning rain and demonic armies. Once he overcame all of these challenges, he awakened to the reality that everything in the universe is caused and that all things are subject to the laws of cause and effect and therefore connected.

Saint Theresa of Avila: Theresa, a 16th-century Catholic nun, was a devout meditator, who often skirted with Catholic doctrine due to her insistence that through deep contemplation freedom and God could be found within us. In her book *The Way of Perfection*, she wrote: "We need no wings to go in search of God, but have only to find a place where we can be alone and look upon Him present within us."

The ancient traditions and practice of mysticism and mindfulness continue today, and many people considered famous in our era continue the practice so essential and fundamental to meditators of the past. The practice today is as relevant now as it was then.

Media personality Oprah Winfrey: Oprah Winfrey is a major advocate of mindfulness, practices daily, and lectures as to its healing power. She has said; "Prayer is you speaking to God. Meditation is allowing the spirit to speak to you."

Professional basketball player Kobe Bryant: Kobe states that he meditates every day in order to clear his mind, which allows him to focus on critical moments in the game. He says, "Meditation is my anchor that allows me to deal with whatever comes my way."

Publisher Arianna Huffington: As one of the most successful people in publishing, she had known about mindfulness, but it was after collapsing from exhaustion that she recognized that it had to become a mainstay of each day. She writes: "The difference now is a consistent prioritizing in my life. It doesn't mean that I do it perfectly by any means. But it is very much part of my life every day."

U.S. representative Tim Ryan: The Democratic representative from Ohio became a devotee of mindfulness after attending a retreat with Kabat-Zinn. He wrote the book *Mindful Nation* with a foreword written by former president Bill Clinton. Ryan said in an interview: "The more I researched it, the more I realized: if this is presented as something that's universal, everyone can benefit. Football players, marines, my constituents—this is for everybody."

NBA coaching great Phil Jackson: He states that with the "ability to step back and observe your experience in an uncritical way, you can actually understand how your mind works, how your body works, how the universe works, how basketball works, and also understanding that when you're performing at your best level, there's usually a lack of self-consciousness." He has attributed much of the success of his teams to the addition of mindfulness practice.

Apple founder Steve Jobs: In her book *Thrive* Arianna Huffington quotes Steve Jobs as loving meditation. "If you just sit and observe, you will see how restless your mind is. If you try to calm it, it only makes it worse, but over time it does calm, and when it does, there's room to hear more subtle things—that's when your intuition starts to blossom and you start to see things more clearly and be in the present more. Your mind just slows down, and you see a tremendous expanse in the moment. You see so much more than you could see before."

Comedian Jerry Seinfeld: In various interviews, Seinfeld has said that he has been practicing meditation for over 40 years. He was filming up to 24 episodes of his eponymous show a year and states, "I'm just a normal guy. And that was not a normal situation to be in. . . . So I meditated every day. And that's how I survived the nine years."

Singer Katy Perry: In a 2015 interview with *Rolling Stone* magazine, Perry said that she starts each day with meditation to help her get into a positive state of mind. "It's changed the way I've thought about things and it's changed my attitude. You know how you have a crappy day and something just doesn't want to go right? I always excuse myself for 20 minutes and then I'm back."

Actor Hugh Jackman: In an interview with psychiatrist Dr. Norman Rosenthal, Jackman says: "I found that with meditation, my anxiety levels dropped considerably. It seems to me that the mind is fuel to the fire of fear. The mind can make us worry about things beyond their measure. And the great thing about meditation is that twice a day, the monkey mind just calms down."

Baseball legend Derek Jeter: The Yankees famed shortstop kept an online diary known as *The Captain's Log*. He used mindfulness as a way to focus his attention.

There are many other people in positions of power who are publicly known to use mindfulness today and find this ancient practice to be relevant in their lives today.

❖❖❖

Research and Applications

25. How is research on mindfulness conducted?

Because mindfulness works across so many domains of health, the scientific community has increasingly begun to dig deep into the numerous brain networks and other biological changes that occur while a person is meditating. There are specific brain areas that mindfulness appears to impact, and certain blood tests also show changes during mindfulness. Whereas blood tests are relatively easy to do, brain scans are more complicated to carry out and then interpret. Further, because brain-imaging research is in its infancy and because different types of mindfulness activate different parts of the brain, many more studies will need to be completed in order to get a clearer impact on how mindfulness affects the brain.

Zen practice typically tends to involve undirected awareness of the present moment, whereas *Vipassana* meditation tends to be much more focused, such as on the breath or body sensations; it is not clear that all practices will lead to similar changes. This is true for many other of life's pursuits. Practicing piano will not make a person good at violin, doing pushups may develop a person's chest but do little for the leg muscles, and so on. Different meditative practices might change different areas of the brain, and scientific research is attempting to look at whether there are changes and if so what they are.

RELEVANT BRAIN ANATOMY

The *amygdala* is an almond-shaped collection of brain cells, also known as neurons, deep inside the brain. It processes emotional information, meaning that emotions triggered by a specific situation are then experienced. The amygdala is best known for managing the fear response, which is also known as the *fight-or-flight response*. People with very strong emotions have very active amygdalae, and so the emotional responses that arise tend to be big. The amygdala also plays an important role in the making of memories, in particular, memories tied to strong emotions. This is a critical function that, under normal circumstances, allows for a fear experience—like being bitten by a stray dog—to be registered and stored in memory, in this case making it less likely that a person will go up to stray dogs in the future.

The prefrontal cortex (PFC) is the part of the brain located directly behind the forehead. It is responsible for controlling what are known as executive functions, which include mediating conflicting thoughts, making choices between right and wrong or good and bad, predicting future events based on current behaviors, and controlling social behavior in group settings.

The ability to measure what is going on in the brain during specific activities, including mindfulness, is done by looking at the signals produced by changes in blood flow, blood oxygen, and blood sugar in the part of the brain being used. Specifically, the technique most commonly used is *functional magnetic resonance imaging* or *functional* (fMRI), which uses an MRI brain scanner to measure brain activity by tracking changes in blood flow during specific brain activities. This technique relies on the fact that blood, which carries oxygen and sugar, flows to the part of the brain that is being used. This is no different than when blood flows to the muscles being used during specific exercises.

Another type of MRI is known as *structural magnetic resonance imaging*. Different from functional scans, which measure activity, structural scans look at the actual structure of the brain and more specifically how much gray or white matter is present in different parts of the brain. Gray matter is where the actual brain activity is processed, and people who have work that requires a lot of thinking will tend to have more gray matter. White matter is the neurons that allow for communication and connection between the different parts of the brain.

Magnetic resonance spectroscopy of the brain looks at the actual chemical reactions taking place at the level of the individual nerve bundles.

Positron emission tomography scans involve the injection of a very small dose of a radioactive chemical into the bloodstream. The chemical then attaches to brain receptors, and the radioactivity of the chemicals is then measured to give an indication of the level of activity in that part of the brain.

There are now thousands of studies on brain scanning findings in people who meditate, and it is beyond the scope of this book to look at all of them and the effects on the brain. A recent study (Hasenkamp & Barsalou, 2012) that looked at the ways in which the brain functions during four different mental states during meditation showed that each mental state was associated with changes in different brain networks. Typically, most researchers would look at the changes in these areas as mental states change during mindfulness.

1. During focus on the present moment, there was activity in the dorsolateral prefrontal cortex.
2. Mind-wandering was associated with activity in an area of the brain known as the default mode network.
3. Awareness of mind-wandering was associated with activity in what is known as the salience network.
4. Finally, a shift of attention back toward focus on the present moment was linked to activity in the right dorsolateral prefrontal cortex.

As an example of one of the thousands of studies using brain imaging, researchers (Holzel et al., 2016) looked at the effects of meditation on the fear networks in the brain. MRI scans show that after an eight-week course of mindfulness practice, the amygdala begins to shrink, and then as the amygdala shrinks, the PFC becomes thicker. While this is happening, the connection between the amygdala and the rest of the brain weakens, while the connections within the PFC strengthen. Further, the amount of change in these brain structures is directly correlated to the number of hours of mindfulness practice a person has done.

Another way to study the effects of mindfulness is to look at what happens to the body's chemistry by examining blood tests, for instance.

Cortisol is a chemical released during stress that helps to break down carbohydrates and proteins in order to increase the supply of glucose and oxygen to the muscles, the heart, and the brain. However, when levels of cortisol are too high, as occurs during time of high stress, this leads to a series of adverse effects, including an increase in blood pressure, an increase in sugar levels, unhealthy abdominal fat buildup, weakening of the bones, a poorly functioning immune system, more rapid aging, and damage to the hippocampus, the brain's primary memory center.

A number of studies have demonstrated reductions in cortisol subsequent to mindfulness interventions (Lipschitz, Kuhn, Kinney, Donaldson, & Nakamura, 2013), and other research (Brand, Holsboer-Trachsler, Naranjo, & Schmidt, 2012) showed that participating in an MBSR program decreased cortisol levels for both experienced and novice meditators.

C-reactive protein (CRP) is a protein that increases in the blood during illness states. It is commonly found in elevated levels in all types of conditions, including major depression. Typically, when a person recovers from illness, his or her CRP levels go back down to normal levels. In a study (Eisendrath et al., 2016) researchers found that using only mindfulness-based cognitive therapy and no other treatment in people with depression resulted in significant decreases in CRP levels as well as reductions in depression severity ratings.

As brain scanning and imaging continues to improve, our ability to search deeper into the brain will significantly enhance our ability to more reliably understand the specific brain circuits, chemicals, and mechanisms by which mindfulness works.

26. What does research show about mindfulness and interpersonal relationships?

Beyond the benefits to the individual, mindfulness has been shown to have a positive impact on interpersonal relationships. Although many research studies focus on conflicted relationships, there is data that even in those not in conflict, couples who practice mindfulness see improvements in their relationships. The benefits include an increase in happiness and a decrease in relationship stress.

Very few relationships cause more emotional distress than the pain of conflict with an intimate or romantic partner. This is because intimacy forces a person to be vulnerable. Vulnerability brings with it trust but also can lead to anxiety and the fear of being rejected or exposed. A 2004 research group at the University of North Carolina studied what it termed "relative happy, non-distressed couples." It adapted the mindfulness-based stress reduction (MBSR) to couples based on the idea that healthy individual functioning is important to successful marriages. It compared 22 couples in the study to 22 couples on a waitlist. The couples had to have been married for at least 12 months and could not be practicing meditation or yoga. Given that these couples were already happy, any enhancement in their relationships would be significant. The researchers found that the more mindfulness was practiced on a particular day, the more the couples experienced improved levels of relationship happiness and reduced levels of relationship stress. These benefits were observed on the day of mindfulness practice and for several consecutive days afterward.

It not only impacts romantic relationships. When parents aren't able to help their children in physical, emotional, and cognitive domains, the children are at significantly increased risk for behavioral problems. Mindfulness has been studied as a way to enhance parenting. In 2015, research by Dr. Douglas Coatsworth and colleagues sought to integrate mindfulness training with parents into a program known as Strengthening Families Program (SFP), an empirically validated family-based preventive intervention. They randomly divided 432 families into two groups. The purpose was to test the effectiveness of adding mindfulness to the program and they called it Mindfulness-Enhanced Strengthening Families Program (MSFP). They compared the results of parent–child relationships to a group that received the standard SFP. The researchers found that MSFP was as effective as SFP in improving many aspects of parenting, including interpersonal mindfulness in parenting, the quality of the relationship between parent and child, an improved ability to manage the child's behavior youth, and overall parent well-being. These results were endorsed by both parents and children and continued for a year after the mindfulness intervention.

Beyond romantic and family relationships, mindfulness can help at work. The majority of employees work in positions that require them to interact directly with customers, colleagues, or clients regardless of the type of work they do. In their jobs, many people experience emotionally charged encounters, conflict with supervisors and supervisees, and these interactions can lead to employees becoming emotionally exhausted and then lead to burnout, resentment, and reduced job satisfaction.

In two 2013 studies conducted by psychologist Ute Hülsheger and her colleagues, the researchers looked first at a five-day diary study with 219 employees in all different work sectors, including nurses, teachers, office clerks, and human resource consultants. The diary study asked the participants, employees who had never been trained in mindfulness, to answer questions as to how they paid attention to daily interactions. They found that the more mindful and present employees were, the less emotional exhaustion and the more job satisfaction they experienced. In the second study 64 employees were randomly divided into two groups: a group that practiced a self-training mindfulness intervention and a control group. The results showed that those in the mindfulness intervention group experienced significantly less emotional exhaustion and more job satisfaction than the employees in the control group.

Mindfulness also helps in therapy relationships. Research shows that the single most important factor in psychotherapy, no matter what its form, is the relationship and that a therapeutic relationship character-ized by empathy, warmth, and connectedness is foundational to healing. Researchers have theorized that the best way to improve any therapy is by learning to improve therapists' ability to relate to their patients and thereby to tailor interventions to the specific needs of individual patients. Further, research has shown that effective therapists engage less in behav-iors, such as blaming the patient, ignoring their requests, rejecting their perspectives, or insisting on a specific technique when their patients don't appear to be benefiting.

In a 2007 study by Dr. Shauna Shapiro and colleagues, the researchers compared masters-level therapists in training to an active control group. The study group completed an eight-week standard MBSR program. The therapists in the MBSR group showed significant improvement on various outcomes as compared to the control group, including decreases in stress, anxiety, and rumination as well as increases in positive mood states.

Many studies show that mindfulness helps the therapists, but what about the impact of therapists practicing mindfulness on the relationship with their patient from the patient's point of view? This was researched in 2016 by psychologist Dr. Patricia Lynn Dobkin and colleagues at McGill University, who found that therapists experienced the benefits of the Sha-piro study, and then when the patients were asked about the effect of their clinicians' practice of mindfulness, they noted that the patient-centered care improved after MBSR. Patients also reported that their therapists had a markedly better understanding of their experience of their illness.

27. What does research show about mindfulness and specific mental disorders?

Mindfulness practice has been shown to positively influence psycholog-ical states whether a person has a mental health condition or not. Over the past few years research on mindfulness in specific psychological disor-ders has exploded, and the evidence of the efficacy of mindfulness-based treatments continues to grow. According to the National Institute of Health's PubMed database, there are close to 500 scientific studies on mindfulness and meditation and the brain. The positive outcomes have made the practice more accepted as an added tool for mental well-being and healing.

MAJOR TECHNIQUES

Mindfulness-based stress reduction (MBSR): MBSR was developed by psychiatrist Jon Kabat-Zinn at the University of Massachusetts. It is based on education about stress and training in coping strategies and assertiveness. The mindfulness component includes seated meditation, body scans—which are assessment of the practitioner's own body state, and hatha yoga. It has been incorporated in multiple physical illness states.

Mindfulness-based cognitive therapy (MBCT): MBCT is derived from MBSR and typically involves eight weekly, two-hour group training sessions, daily homework assignments, yoga stretching, and follow-up meetings. Homework assignments include mindfulness exercises and using mindfulness skills in everyday life. MBCT combines cognitive behavior techniques with mindfulness techniques, breathing exercises, and stretching to target the cycle of negative thoughts which are common in people with recurrent episodes of depression.

Dialectical behavior therapy (DBT): Mindfulness is the foundational skill of DBT. It is a treatment that uses mindfulness to then access other behavioral skills to reduce self-destructive and suicidal behaviors.

Acceptance and commitment therapy (ACT): ACT is another evidence-based psychological intervention that uses mindfulness strategies, together with acceptance strategies and commitment as well as behavior change strategies, to increase psychological flexibility or the ability to be in the present moment and then, based on what the situation affords, making the choice to change or persist in whatever behavior in the service of a person's chosen values.

Mindfulness-based relapse prevention (MBRP): MBRP was developed to treat substance use disorder. It integrates mindfulness and cognitive behavior skills specifically focused on helping patients learn to choose a behavior instead of automatically turning to an addictive substance. Similar to MBSR and MBCT, it involves eight weekly, two-hour group training sessions, daily home exercises, and follow-up.

CONDITIONS TREATED

Anxiety

Dr. Samuel Wong and colleagues (2016) studied the effects of MBCT when compared with treatment as usual (TAU) and cognitive behavioral therapy-based psycho-education in 182 patients with generalized anxiety disorder (GAD) and found that MBCT and cognitive behavioral therapy-based psycho-education were superior to TAU in reducing symptoms of anxiety.

Acute Depression

Dr. J. R. van Aalderen of the Department of Psychiatry at Radboud University in the Netherlands looked at the effectiveness of MBCT in people currently in and out of remission of depression (2012). His researchers enrolled 102 participants in an MBCT and compared their outcomes to 103 people who received TAU. They found that patients in the MBCT group reported fewer depressive symptoms, as well as less worry and rumination and increased levels of mindfulness ability compared with patients who received TAU alone. Their analysis suggested that the benefit was mediated by decreased levels of rumination and worry.

Recurrent Depression

In a thorough review of multiple studies on preventing the relapse of depression, research headed by Dr. Willem Kuyken at Oxford (2016) found that MBCT was useful in helping prevent recurrence of depression, particularly for patients with more severe depression. Their research showed that patients receiving MBCT had a reduced risk of depressive relapse within a 60-week follow-up period compared with those who did not receive MBCT.

Substance Abuse

Psychologist Sarah Bowen and colleagues (2014) compared TAU to MBRP and cognitive behavioral relapse prevention (RP) in 286 patients who had completed acute treatment for substance abuse. They found that compared to TAU those assigned to the MBRP and RP arms of the study reported significantly lower risk of relapse to substance use, including heavy drinking, and, among those who used substances, significantly fewer days of substance use and heavy drinking when they were followed up after six months. Cognitive behavioral RP showed an advantage over MBRP in time to first drug use; however, at the 12-month follow-up, the MBRP participants reported significantly fewer days of substance use and significantly decreased heavy drinking compared with RP and TAU.

Attention Deficit Hyperactivity Disorder (ADHD)

A study by Dr. Saskia van der Oord at the University of Amsterdam (2012) studied the effects of mindfulness on 11 children aged 8–12 years and the impact of mindful parenting on their parents. The researchers found that the children's ADHD symptoms decreased significantly after mindfulness training for the entire family. They noted that parental mindfulness was likely a key part of helping children with ADHD learn to manage their symptoms.

Post-Traumatic Stress Disorder (PTSD)

Psychologist Kathi Heffner at the University of Rochester looked at the effects of mindfulness training for veterans diagnosed with PTSD (2016). Heffner compared TAU with various forms of mindfulness training in 391 male and female veterans at six different Veterans Administration (VA) sites. The types of meditation used were sitting mindfulness, transcendental meditation, and mantra meditation. The TAU was other evidence-based treatments for trauma: prolonged exposure and present-centered therapy. The researchers found positive benefits in the mindfulness and mantra programs and recommended that these approaches be included in treating veterans with PTSD.

Borderline Personality Disorder

Dr. Albert Feliu-Soler and colleagues (2014) looked at the effects of DBT mindfulness training on emotional reactivity in people with borderline personality disorder (BPD). They added 10 weeks of DBT-mindfulness (DBT-M) training to another treatment known as general psychiatric management (GPM) in order to assess if the addition of mindfulness could improve emotion regulation in a study of 35 patients with BPD. A total of 35 patients were divided into GPM alone and compared to patients receiving both GPM and DBT-M. The patients in the DBT-M group showed greater improvement in clinical symptoms. The formal mindfulness practice was positively associated with clinical improvements and lower self-reported emotional reactivity.

Beyond the aforementioned conditions, mindfulness-based approaches are being studied in many other mental health conditions, including psychosis, emotion regulation, bipolar disorder, phobias, relationship difficulties, and sleep problems, and over time, research will show if mindfulness similarly improves outcomes of these other disorders.

28. Is there any research on the physical health benefits of mindfulness?

Most of the research on the impact of mindfulness on physical well-being has been done on the application known as *mindfulness-based stress reduction* (MBSR), a system that uses mindfulness meditation to alleviate the suffering associated with physical and mental health disorders. In the past two decades, a number of research reports have looked at the various ways in which the technique has positively impacted physical health.

In a review of all of the studies at the time (2004), Professor Paul Grossman at Freiburg Institute for Mindfulness Research reviewed 20 reports, with 1,605 study participants. He found that mindfulness training was being used in medical patients with many conditions, including fibromyalgia, various cancer types, coronary artery diseases, depression, chronic pain, anxiety, obesity, and binge eating disorder. There is currently so much research on mindfulness in various medical conditions that it is beyond the scope of this book, so the following review is a tiny sample of all the research.

PAIN

Dr. Lance McCracken at King's College, London, studied the benefits of the mindfulness-based acceptance and commitment therapy (ACT) for chronic pain in several studies. The first study (2005) looked studied 108 chronic pain patients who completed a three- to four-week residential pain program. The study participants reported increases in emotional, social, and physical functioning and needed less medical interventions. His team then repeated the treatment in a new group of 171 chronic pain sufferers (2008). They offered three to four weeks of ACT and mindfulness-based treatment in a group format for five days per week for six and a half hours each day. The participants noted significant improvements on their experience of pain, depression, and pain-related anxiety. They also reported feeling less disabled and needed fewer medical visits as well as improved ability for physical performance.

CANCER

In a large meta-analysis of the research on the impact of mindfulness in patients with breast cancer, Dr. Yaowarat Matchim and colleagues (2011) reviewed 16 studies of MBSR conducted with breast cancer survivors. The majority of participants in the 16 studies were early-stage breast cancer survivors. They found that there was most improvement in psychological outcomes, such as perceived stress and anxiety.

Four of the 18 studies looked at biological outcomes, including immune profile, blood pressure, heart rate, cortisol level, and melatonin levels. The researchers found that different from the psychological outcomes, there were less evident improvements in these biological measures.

In other research by Dr. Linda Carlson at the University of Calgary (2007), her team looked at the outcome of an eight-week course in MBSR in 49 patients with breast cancer and 10 with prostate cancer. As when compared to the beginning of the study, after the participants had completed the MBSR, the cancer patients experienced enduring quality-of-life improvements, with a decrease in stress symptoms, lowered cortisol blood levels, and improved immune patterns consistent with both reduced stress and depressed mood and an overall decrease in their blood pressure.

FIBROMYALGIA

Fibromyalgia is a chronic disorder which presents with muscle and joint pain, fatigue, and tenderness in certain body parts. Professor Grossman (2007) and his colleagues looked at the effects of MBSR on a group of 58 women who were then assigned to either MBSR or an active support condition that was not mindfulness based. The women in the MBSR group showed greater improvement from the start of the study and beyond with regard to their experience of pain, coping, quality of life, anxiety, depression, and somatic complaints, and these improvements were still measurable three years later.

CARDIOVASCULAR DISEASE

Dr. Martin Sullivan, a cardiologist from Hendersonville, North Carolina, and colleagues (2009) conducted an interesting study known as SEARCH: The Support, Education, and Research in Chronic Heart Failure Study (SEARCH): a mindfulness-based psychoeducational intervention for patients with depression and heart disease. They assigned 208 patients with chronic heart failure to one of two groups, being either an intervention consisting of mindfulness meditation practice, coping skills, and group discussion for patients who lived close enough to attend the group meetings or a treatment as usual (TAU) group for those who lived too far from the medical center. They found that patients in the mindfulness group had greater reductions in anxiety, depression, and cardiac symptoms immediately after the study as well as after three and six months.

RHEUMATOID ARTHRITIS

Rheumatoid arthritis (RA) is a painful autoimmune condition caused by swelling of the joints. Autoimmune means that a person's immune system sees itself as alien and then sends antibodies to attack its own tissues. There are two important studies looking at the effect of mindfulness on RA.

In the first study (2007), 63 patients were divided into two groups by Dr. Elizabeth Pradhan and colleagues at the University of Maryland. The first group received MBSR, and the second were left on a *waitlist*. Having people on a waitlist is a common research technique: it is a control group, where the group of participants included in the study is assigned to a waiting list, with the understanding that the group will receive the intervention after the active treatment group—in this case MBSR.

After two months, there were *no* differences between the groups on measures of depression, distress, well-being and mindfulness, or the RA disease activity as evaluated by a medical specialist. However, at six months there were significant self-reported improvements in the MBSR group.

In the second study (2008), conducted by Professor Alex Zautra at Arizona State University, 144 participants were randomly assigned to one of three study groups: (1) cognitive behavioral therapy (CBT) for pain, (2) mindfulness meditation and emotion regulation therapy, and (3) education-only. The researchers found the greatest improvements in pain control and the greatest reductions in blood markers of inflammation in the group receiving CBT; however, both the CBT and mindfulness groups improved more in coping than the education control group. Patients with RA and a history of depression benefited more from mindfulness in terms of their mood and on the physicians' ratings of joint tenderness. This suggested that MBSR would be preferable to CBT for treating people with RA and other chronic medical illnesses who also struggle with depression.

DIABETES

There have been quite a few studies on the use of mindfulness-based approaches in diabetes. For instance, Dr. Steven Rosenzweig conducted a study (2007) in 11 patients with type 2 diabetes and looked at the impact of MBSR on measures of blood sugar control. This is significant as stress has been related to poorer control of blood sugar levels in people with type 2 diabetes. At one month following the start of the MBSR program, glycosylated hemoglobin A1C (HbA1C), which is a blood test that measures blood sugar levels, was significantly reduced. The group of patients doing the MBSR also had lower blood pressure, lower depression, lower anxiety, and lower overall psychological distress.

HIV

In a study on the effects of mindfulness on HIV outcomes (2009) Dr. David Cresswell and his colleagues assigned 48 HIV-infected adults to two groups: either an eight-week MBSR class or a one-day stress reduction education seminar. The one-day seminar group was in order to compare MBSR and non-MBSR. They measured levels of the blood cells known as CD4+ T lymphocytes. CD4 cells also known as T-helper cells are a type of white blood cells that are essential in fighting viruses. In the control group, the CD4 cells decreased substantially; however, they remained stable in the MBSR group. Interestingly, people with HIV who attended more of the MBSR classes showed more stability in their CD4 counts.

IRRITABLE BOWEL SYNDROME

A Swedish group led by Dr. Brjánn Ljótsson (2011) looked at an online adapted version of their acceptance and mindfulness-based intervention with 61 patients with irritable bowel syndrome (IBS) and compared the intervention to patients on a waitlist. The patients received the intervention through weekly contact with their therapists by e-mail. The mindfulness group had to work through five successive therapeutic steps and was not able to move to the next step until they had completed the previous step. Compared to those on the waitlist, the mindfulness participants had better quality of life, reduced IBS symptoms, and reduced IBS-related fear and avoidance behaviors. These gains were maintained over the next 12 months after completion of the study. Of further interest was that the mindfulness intervention was more cost-effective than the waiting list.

29. Can mindfulness help in sports?

So other than being champions in their field of sports, what do the Super Bowl champions Seattle Seahawks, Olympic snowboarder Gretchen Bleiler, basketball great Kobe Bryant, the Olympic BMX cycling team, professional tennis player Novak Djokovic, and many other elite sports teams and athletes have in common? All have introduced mindfulness as a way to compete better through improving their capacity to focus their attention to the present moment.

An aphorism tells us that performance in sports is 90 percent mental. Yet most time and money is spent on the physical aspect of the sport, whether it is paying for trainers or equipment or practicing on the field. Very little time is spent on the mental aspects of the game.

The field of sports psychology has been around for more than 100 years and according to Dr. Robert Weinberg at the University of Miami (2010) involves "the study of how psychological factors affect performance and how participation in sport and exercise affect psychological and physical factors." Typically, sports psychologists focus on visualizing the moment, making positive self-statements, and challenging negative self-talk. In fact, many of the traditional mental training strategies are based on classical cognitive behavioral assumption that negative thoughts about the self-need to be changed or stopped altogether in order to optimize performance.

It turns out that trying to change such negative thinking means that the focus is on negativity, and this can lead to increasing the frequency and focus on such thoughts which can in turn lead to a worsening of performance according to research by Drs. Richard Wenzlaff and Daniel Wegner (2000). Therefore, rather than trying to control or eliminate such thoughts, athletes benefit more from developing the capacity for present-moment awareness and nonjudgmental acceptance of negative thoughts and emotions. This paradigm shift is the central underpinning of all mindfulness-based interventions.

Todays' champions are going beyond positive self-talk and including the practices of mindfulness, meditation, and yoga into their training regimen. As in other endeavors, the athletes learn to stay focused on the present moment, with specific attention to the connection between the mind and the body.

For instance, Djokovic describes his practice in his book *Serve to Win* (2013). He writes that he practices mindfulness "every day for about fifteen minutes, and it is as important to me as my physical training."

Recently, an elite tennis player asked me for help with her game. She overwhelmed most of her rivals at a local level, but once she started to compete with nationally ranked players, she said: "I become discouraged before I even start, I tell myself that I can't do it, that I can't beat my opponent, that I am too anxious and that I can't focus. My heart starts to pound and my mouth gets dry." Her case is not unusual. Most athletes will notice some level of worry during competition. That is normal. What makes the great ones great is the ability to control and moderate the level of stress that they experience.

By bringing the practice of mindfulness to the experience on the sports field, in the case of my client the tennis court, the athlete learns to respond to what is actually happening over the anxieties and fears of what she thinks might happen.

Mindfulness first trains the prefrontal cortex to stay focused and reduce distractions. It reduces stress and allows emotions to pass quickly. At a brain cell level, it takes less than 90 seconds for an emotion to get triggered, for the chemicals associated with that emotion to surge through the body before the chemicals flush out. However, many people feel that their emotions last much longer, and the reason they do so is rumination. Rumination is the behavior of compulsively focusing attention on the experience of distress and playing a scenario over and over. An example of rumination would be tennis players who spend minutes replaying a past point in their head, thinking about what they should have done rather than staying present in the moment of the current point.

Mindfulness also helps reduce an excess of stress chemicals, which can reduce physical performance. Earlier we discussed the effects of mindfulness in terms of reducing cortisol. Cortisol is released by the adrenal glands under conditions of high mental and physical stress. The three main functions of cortisol are to reduce buildup of protein, increase the breakdown of protein, and stop tissue growth. Cortisol, therefore, has an adverse effect on muscle growth, the exact opposite effect of what an athlete wants, and so it is essential that cortisol release be controlled in order to reduce the ill effects of stress and facilitate muscle growth.

Finally, through bringing attention inward, the part of the brain known as the insular cortex is activated. The insular cortex is the part of the brain responsible for consciousness. As a result athletes experience a heightened sense of awareness of their body in space and motion, allowing for improved communication between the body and mind. For instance, mindful awareness that a muscle is tense or that breathing is excessive will allow for adjustments in the moments.

The first research of mindfulness for athletes was undertaken by Dr. Kabat-Zinn in 1985. The research found that with mindfulness training, a group of college rowers performed well above their coach's expectations. Further, a group of Olympic rowers reported feeling that the mindfulness had enhanced their performance. The rowers also noted increases in concentration and relaxation and a reduction in negative thoughts and fatigue. Even with this early evidence of a powerful performance-enhancing practice, it took nearly 20 years before mindfulness was incorporated as mainstream. There are two research-supported, mindfulness-based approaches for athletes. The first is known as mindfulness-acceptance-commitment

(MAC) developed by Drs. Frank Gardner and Zella Moore in 2001. The second is known as mindful sport performance enhancement (MSPE) developed by Drs. Keith Kaufman and Carol Glass in 2006.

> MAC: The MAC method combines mindfulness exercises with acceptance techniques with a focus on enhancing performance through the promotion of a nonjudgmental, present-moment awareness and acceptance of the athlete's thoughts and emotional state. The approach also promotes focused attention to the performance task and includes an intentional, values-driven commitment to behaviors that support athletic goals (Gardner & Moore, 2012). Values-driven commitment means that athletes focus on behaviors that are consistent with their personal goals in all endeavors of their life. For instance, even though drinking alcohol might not have anything to do with their sport; they might incorporate not drinking as a way of focusing on overall health. MAC emphasizes reducing judgmental labeling of events, thoughts, and emotions. By mindfully increasing attention to such thoughts, the athlete then learns to let the thoughts go.
>
> MSPE: MSPE teaches athletes how to apply mindfulness skills to sport through repeated practice and then discussion of mindfulness exercises. It also focuses having the athlete train in exercises that target the cultivation of mindfulness, for instance, sitting meditation, body scans, mindful yoga, and walking meditation. MSPE also adds a walking meditation adapted to be specific to fundamental movements involved in the sport of the individual. MSPE was initially applied to archers and golfers, both of which are individual sports that require tremendous focus. In the original studies, the archers' overall ability to stay mindful and be confident increased significantly. Golfers, in turn, showed a significant increase in their ability to describe the situation as it really was. The majority (more than 75%) of athletes using the MSPE method reported that the mindfulness training would increase their performance and enjoyment of their respective sports.

Like MAC, MSPE emphasizes the development of mindfulness skills. Unlike MAC, MSPE does not include a focus on values, value-driven behavior, or commitment.

> MAC: MAC was demonstrated as effective in a pair of case studies: one with a female bodybuilder and another with a male swimmer (Gardner & Moore, 2004). Both athletes in the case studies achieved

personal bests. Then in a 2005 study by Gardner using Division I collegiate field hockey and volleyball players, the researchers reported a noticeable but small treatment effect similar to traditional psychological skills training. Dr. Andrew Wolanin at La Salle University (2005) conducted an open trial of MAC and reported an increase in self and coach ratings of performance, as well as self and coach ratings of attention and practice intensity when compared to athletes who did not use MAC.

MSPE: Dr. Rachel Thompson and colleagues at the Catholic University of America (2011) reviewed the long-term effects of MSPE on various sports. They reported on a one-year follow-up of MSPE with assessments conducted on archers, golfers, and long-distance runners who had attended MSPE workshops. They found that across the athlete groups, the participants reported significant increases in the ability to act with awareness as when compared to before the training. The athletes also reported significant decreases in sport-related worries and sport-irrelevant thoughts, both of which are ways in which thoughts interfere with performance. The long-distance runners showed significant improvement in their mile times from before MSPE to follow-up, with significant correlation between their overall improvement and ability for mindfulness.

As in other life endeavors, mindfulness appears to have an enhancing effect on athletic performance and productivity together with increasing an overall sense of satisfaction in the sport.

30. Can mindfulness help in academics?

Given the evidence that mindfulness helps in diverse human enterprises, it is no surprise that it has been researched and applied to the field of education. There is a significant connection between stress, poor emotional regulation, and poor life prospects, and today's students are more stressed than they have ever been. The first efforts to use mindfulness in schools began in the United Kingdom in 2007. Since then it has spread across the world, and today many schools have mindfulness curricula for teachers and students. In the United States the two most widespread approaches are MindUP and Mindful Schools.

Early life stress can lead to a domino effect where stress leads to disruption in *executive function*—the brain's ability to plan, organize, and complete tasks. These skills are obviously essential to education, and when disrupted, the consequence for the child is poor self-control and ineffective emotion regulation. This then leads to a poor ability to tolerate distress and the challenges of the school day, and then behavioral outbursts mean that not only is the child incapable of learning, but then by getting kicked out of the classroom and being placed in detention this further removes the child from the academic setting. The child then gets the reputation of being a disruptive student and then begins to believe the narrative that he or she is incapable of succeeding, in turn leading to poor self-esteem. Historically, the U.S. educational system has focused on test scores and cognitive intelligence at the expense of emotional wellness and emotional intelligence, dimensions of personhood that are difficult to measure in tests and quizzes. When a system focuses only on academics at the expense of emotional wellness, the child suffers because the foundation of a fulfilling life lies less in academics grades than in the capacity for emotion regulation, resilience, and interpersonal effectiveness, all targets of mindfulness.

There are many areas in which mindfulness can be applied to the school setting, for instance, *test anxiety* where physical and behavioral reactions associated with the worry of getting poor grades can impact performance on a test. With competition for college placement increasing and with employers demanding better educated employees, the emphasis on academic and standardized testing has increased. Professor Jerrell Cassady reported the impact of test anxiety on exam performance (2002) and noted that the anxiety could arise from worry about the course material, fear of disappointing parents, the fear of doing poorly, and worry about the consequences of getting poor grades.

In a 2010 research paper on test anxiety, Prima Vitasari and colleagues showed that test anxiety had negative effects on memory span, concentration, and reasoning. Digging deeper into the brain, anxiety significantly impacts what is known as *working memory*, which is the neural network that uses attention to focus on relevant information and block any irrelevant information, which might arise from distracting thoughts. It is an immediate form of memory important for problem solving, reasoning, and reading comprehension in the moment.

In order to examine the effects of mindfulness on working memory, Dr. Michael Mrazek at the University of California, Santa Barbara, noted that a distracted mind, one that switches the focus of its attention to nontask-related worries such as environmental stressors, negatively impacted academic performance. His group investigated (2013) whether a two-week mindfulness training course would decrease mind-wandering and improve cognitive performance and found a significant improvement in reading-comprehension scores and working memory capacity while reducing the occurrence of worry while the research subjects were studying for exams. They found that the improvement in the students' performance and test results was because of their increased ability to focus and a reduction in distractions caused by worry thoughts.

Many have been skeptical of the utility of mindfulness in schools, and some see it as a waste of time taking students away from time that could be spent learning. Others have wanted to block its application on religious grounds. It is the mistaken belief that mindfulness is introducing a spiritual practices into their kids' lives, one not in keeping with their own religious beliefs. Because of this, various groups have set out to study the effects of their mindfulness method.

"Mindful Schools" is an approach that has been adopted throughout the United States and, in particular, targets underprivileged students. The system teaches teachers mindfulness skills in order to target self-care and ways to connect with young people. Their system has been used to reach nearly a million students; however, recognizing that there has been skepticism, they have been researching their method over the past few years. They partnered with the University of California at Davis and conducted a randomized controlled study of three elementary schools in Oakland, California (Smith, Guzman-Alvarez, Westover, Keller, & Fuller, 2012).

In the study, the researchers taught mindfulness for 15 minutes, three times a week, in some classrooms but not others. They found that in the mindfulness-taught classrooms there were significant improvements: students' behavior improved, as did their ability to focus. Further, the teachers' sense of well-being was enhanced.

MindUP is a mindfulness approach for schools with the goal of helping students to develop emotional self-regulation by teaching children focused breathing exercises while they also practice nonjudgmental awareness of thoughts. As with many mindfulness practices, the hope is to reduce stress, develop techniques for students to calm down, and be less anxious. Professor Kimberly A. Schonert-Reichl at the University of British Columbia (2015) studied 100 fourth and fifth graders who had been divided into two groups. One group received four months of the MindUP curriculum, and the other received a standard "social responsibility" program. At the end of the research, Schonert-Reichl found that the group who had been in the mindfulness arm of the study had 15 percent better math scores, had 24 percent more social behaviors, and were 24 percent less aggressive. Schonert-Reichl concluded that mindfulness helped the children in their study improve their cognitive control while reducing stress. They also become kinder to others by improved ability to take others' perspective and show greater empathy, and the children also self-reported fewer symptoms of depression. Finally, their peers reported that the children who had practiced mindfulness were more pro-social.

31. Can mindfulness help in the business world?

What do the companies Google, the *Huffington*, Intel, Goldman Sachs, Target, and General Mills have in common? Other than being massive multinational companies with hundreds of thousands of employees, they have all recognized the toxic effects of worker stress and added mindfulness to their employee health benefits. This is not surprising. According to the American Psychological Association's 2016 Work and Well-Being Survey, one in three working Americans report being stressed on the job. This is because the demands of work life are interfering with the capacity to stop and think, and with this stress workers are finding less time to exercise or to relax. All of this can impact the decision-making process of the typical employee.

Before this report, in 2009 a conference looking at the problem of stress in the workplace was held in San Francisco. The first conference attracted 325 people. The conference became known as Wisdom 2.0, and by 2012 the conference had speakers, including the founders of companies like Twitter, Facebook, eBay, and PayPal. More specifically, Ford chairman Bill Ford, Arianna Huffington, founder of the *Huffington Post*, LinkedIn CEO Jeff Weiner, and Congressman Tim Ryan all spoke. By 2016 the conference attracted more than 2,500 attendees and people from more than 20 countries.

There are multiple articles written on mindfulness in business magazines like *Forbes* and *The Economist*, and yet despite the remarkable growth and interest in the practice, and the ever-growing number of studies done in multiple domains, there are few robust studies done on the effects of the practice. As of the time of the writing of this book, only two research studies (2013, 2014) on mindfulness in the workplace have been published, and both by psychologist Ute Hülsheger and colleagues at the Department of Work and Social Psychology at Maastricht University in the Netherlands.

In the first study Hülsheger and colleagues found that mindfulness promoted job satisfaction and helped in the prevention of burnout from emotional exhaustion. In the second study they found that workers who practice mindfulness at work had far better sleep quality and ability to let go of work-related worries during off-job times.

Because well-run companies tend to watch their profit line, the cost-effectiveness and wellness effects of various practices including mindfulness have been studied by some of the aforementioned companies, although not necessarily with the rigor of clinical studies. Nevertheless, for instance, the medical insurance company Aetna is one of the largest firms in the United States. The company has more than 50,000 employees. Its CEO is Mark T. Bertolini, who is a regular meditator who decided to offer mindfulness and yoga programs to his workers starting in 2010. As reported by the *New York Times* in a 2015 article, more than 12,000 of his employees took advantage of the program, and they found that those who attended reported, on average, a nearly 30 percent reduction in their stress levels and a 20 percent improvement in sleep quality. The employees become more effective on the job, gaining an hour of productivity time per week, and Aetna estimated that this was worth about $3,000 per employee per year.

Then, the food giant General Mills, well known for the cereal Cheerios and Häagen-Dazs ice cream, completed a seven-week mindfulness and meditation program. It found that more than 80 percent of the workers who did the course said they took time every day to increase their productivity, up from less than 25 percent before the course, and that 80 percent of senior management reported that they had improved their decision-making processes after the course. Importantly, nearly 90 percent said that they had become better listeners.

Although more research needs to be completed, companies are adapting their workplaces to accommodate mindfulness. For instance, at Salesforce.com CEO Marc Benioff decided to outfit the company's new offices with spaces dedicated to promote employees' well-being. In its tower in downtown San Francisco, individual rooms on each floor have been installed, where employees can step away from the intensity of their work in order to practice mindfulness. The *Huffington Post* similarly has space dedicated to mindfulness at its corporate offices, and then Google has used an internal mindfulness program for its employees called Search Inside Yourself. It includes walking meditation and mindful lunches to cultivate mindful practice and well-being.

32. What does research say about mindful eating?

That humans cannot live without food almost goes without saying, but what is less obvious is the relationship to the food we eat. As with all the other ways in which mindfulness can be applied to various aspects of life's endeavors, mindful eating is the idea of bringing awareness to hunger cues, the choice of food, and the use of various senses in eating food and then the effects of having eaten.

Many people will have had the experience of going to the movies and buying a large bucket of butter-covered popcorn, sitting engrossed in the theater, and then leaving with the bucket completely empty, or, alternatively, sitting at the computer, facing a list of e-mails or on social media, with a bowl of chips, large sugary soda, bulging egg salad sandwich, and then with all attention on the screen and much less on the food, within a few bites, all the food is gone. Assuming that the popcorn, chips, soda, and sandwich are food items that the person wants to eat, at a minimum doing other things while eating means that the pleasure of savoring these desired foods is lost to the attentional focus on the movie or the computer screen. More significant, however, is that such mindlessness in eating means that the amount of food is not monitored and the risk of obesity increases significantly.

Because in the developed world the ready and easy access to highly processed, high-calorie foods means that a person can gulp down large amounts of food in minutes, obesity and the consequences of poor-quality eating choices are significantly affecting the health of societies in the first world. In the third world, on the other hand, it is not to say that the same amount of calories would not be consumed but rather that in order to make a high-calorie meal there is a lot of effort required to, for instance, grind the corn, harvest the vegetables, carry the water, make a fire, and cook the meal. These endeavors are taken for granted by people in the industrialized world but are critical in less-developed societies.

Arguably, the first proponent of mindful eating was the early 20th-century American food faddist Horace Fletcher who earned the nickname "The Great Masticator," by arguing that food should be chewed slowly and repeatedly before being swallowed. He argued that people should not eat before they were "good and hungry," or while angry or sad, that eating slowly and deliberately would bring out the essence of the meal, and that knowing exactly what was in food was critical to good health.

An ever-growing body of research suggests that a slower, more mindful way of eating helps with weight problems, allows for more enjoyment of meals, and steers people away from chemically infused processed food and makes more nutritious food choices.

When mindfulness is applied to eating, it means noticing hunger and fullness cues and, then when eating, attending to the colors, smells, flavors, and textures of food. It means savoring each bite by chewing slowly while getting rid of distractions like TV or eating during movies or sports events and then learning to cope with emotions such as shame, guilt, and anxiety that interfere with the experience and enjoyment of eating.

The process of digesting food involves a complex series of interactions between the gut and the brain, and ordinarily it takes about 20 minutes for the brain to register the experience of fullness. The problem then is that if a person eats too quickly, he or she will consume excess calories way before the brain says "enough." To highlight this point, at an absurd extreme for instance, according to the Guinness Book of Records, in 2014 Takeru Kobayashi of Japan ate 12 hamburgers in just over three minutes, or nearly 4,000 calories in that period of time. It is hard to imagine that he would be able to eat any more given space constraints in his intestines, but given the 20-minute gut–brain message delay, in theory he would still have 17 minutes left of eating before his brain sent him a signal to stop.

Beyond the use of mindfulness in non-illness states, mindfulness has been adapted to help treat people with eating disorders such as binge eating disorder (BED), with type 2 diabetes, and for weight loss. The Mindfulness-Based Eating Awareness Training (MB-EAT) program developed by Dr. Jean Kristeller was derived from MBSR and combines mindful eating, meditation, and group discussions on how awareness can help with a person's behaviors and experiences surrounding food.

According to the National Eating Disorders Association, BED is a "severe, life-threatening and treatable eating disorder characterized by recurrent episodes of eating large quantities of food (often very quickly and to the point of discomfort); a feeling of a loss of control during the binge; experiencing shame, distress or guilt afterwards; and not regularly using unhealthy compensatory measures (e.g., purging) to counter the binge eating. It is the most common eating disorder in the United States."

In one study Dr. Jean Kristeller and colleagues (1999) examined MB-EAT in patients with BED and found that the number of binge-eating episodes among study participants decreased from more than 4 per week to about 1.5 and that many patients at the end of the study no longer met the diagnostic criteria for BED.

In a National Institutes of Health study of 140 subjects using MB-EAT, the participants also experienced reductions in episodes of binge eating as well as a reduction in depressive symptoms. Another study of MB-EAT by Kristeller and colleagues (2011) looking at the effects of the treatment on BED and weight loss found that study participants showed a 7-pound weight loss after ten sessions.

MB-EAT has also been adapted for patients with diabetes. In a study published in the *Journal of the Academy of Nutrition and Dietetics* (2012), patients were divided into two groups. One group used the MB-EAT approach using the mindfulness technique, and the second group received traditional counseling and were taught about diabetes self-management. Patients in the MB-EAT group experienced significant weight loss, improved glycemic control, increased fiber intake, and lower trans-fat and sugar consumption.

In another study by Kristeller's group (2011), MB-EAT was used to treat stress eating and reduce cortisol levels. Obese patients who completed the study experienced significantly lower cortisol levels and decreased anxiety but had no changes in weight from baseline. However, when compared to the group who did not use MB-EAT, the control group had gained a significant amount of weight during the study. In the study the patients who had reported the greatest reduction in stress also had the biggest decreases in abdominal fat.

Mindful eating also appears to benefit cancer survivors. In a 2012 study of patients with prostate cancer, Professor James Carmody and colleagues at the University of Massachusetts Medical School looking at the effects of mindful eating in this group showed that combining education on nutrition, cooking classes, mindfulness, and mindful eating training led to changes in diet that were linked to a lower risk of prostate cancer recurrence. Further, there was a significant connection between the meditation practice at the six-month point of the study and increased vegetable and lower animal product consumption.

Mindful eating programs don't have to be done in the context of group settings. In a 2012 study that looked at a six-week course of mindful eating in restaurants, the study participants showed significant weight loss, a reduction in calories consumed, reduced fat intake, and an increase in self-confidence.

Mindfulness and the
Modern World

33. How does being continually connected to multiple electronic devices impact mindfulness?

The digital classroom is here. Today, students use all forms of devices—computers, tablets, and smartphones—as a way to connect with team members, research papers, and consult with teachers. The downside is that because of their power to also deliver multiple other media, they can be very distracting to students. Students often make the case that they have to be on their devices because that is the way that homework is delivered. At the same time parents complain that it makes it difficult for their children to remain on task. There is little question that there have been tremendous benefits to electronic gadgetry; however, there is also evidence that it impacts the brain and its functioning. The question in the context of mindfulness is whether electronic devices impact the ability to attend and focus.

In humans, from a developmental perspective, the brain is the last organ of the body to become anatomically mature. Full maturation is not complete until a person's mid- to late 20s. During this time the brain circuits control the capacities of focus and attention as well as emotional control and the development of empathy.

Specifically, the prefrontal cortex, the area of the brain that governs focus, emotional regulation, and executive functioning, is the part of the brain most at risk. In order to develop these circuits, a person has to use them, and this is done by participating in sustained episodes of concentration through tasks such as reading, listening, and interacting face to face.

In a well-known study published in 2013 focusing on attention and concentration conducted on more than 1,000 children in New Zealand, neuroscientist Terrie E. Moffitt and her team at Duke University tested children born in 1972 and 1973 regularly for eight years. They measured the children's ability to pay attention and to ignore distractions. They then tracked those same children down at the age of 32 to see how well they had done in life and found that the capacity to concentrate that the children had as youngsters was the strongest predictor of success in later life. They also found that children who, in comparison, had lower self-control as adults were more likely to have poor health, depend on drugs or alcohol, be single parents, and have a criminal record.

The problem is that distractions are now the rule rather than the exceptions. Every day people get e-mails, texts, and Facebook and Snapchat messages. Then there is Twitter, surfing the Web, and all the other things that people need to do. Interestingly, knowing that people have increasingly less capacity for focus, and as a consequence the attentive endurance to get through large amounts of text, text and other messaging and Twitter by design have reinforced the use of fewer words over more. These distractions have cost at a corporate level, and there are estimates that this inability to stay focused costs business billions of dollars a year in lost productivity. Professor Gloria Mark, at the University of California, Irvine, reported in 2005 that a worker distracted by electronic messaging and Web searches can take about 25 minutes to return to the task at hand.

Ironically, what these digital media companies are doing is to develop courses that help sharpen attentional skills. The Nobel Prize–winning neuroscientist Eric Kandel wrote in his book *In Search of Memory* (2007) that only by concentrating intensely can a person link new ideas and facts "meaningfully and systematically with knowledge already well-established in memory." This is difficult to do when there are multiple demands on brain circuits.

Because the capacity of multitasking is prized, the question of whether a person can multitask, that is effectively concentrate on the vast amount of incoming electronic data from multiple devices, is an important one to answer. Researchers at Stanford University's Communication between Humans and Interactive Media Lab gave cognitive tests to 49 people who spent a lot of time on electronic media. They compared the results to 52 people who spent significantly less time on electronic media and in 2009 reported their finding that those who spent less time on electronic media did significantly better on the cognitive tests than those who spent more time. In trying to understand why this was the case, the researchers found that multitaskers couldn't help thinking about the task they *weren't* doing, meaning they are always drawing from all the information in front of them, even if that information is irrelevant to what they need to do. They do not have the capacity to keep relevant and irrelevant separate in their minds.

How does multitasking affect the way a person thinks, learns, remembers, and focuses on and processes information? Research shows that rapid task switching takes a significant toll on the speed and accuracy of trying to track multiple tasks. The costs are twofold: First, there are costs to switching between tasks, in that it takes time and energy to refocus; and second, simply being aware that there are other tasks, such as e-mails, to complete and awaiting a person's attention can distract and disrupt attentional circuits even if a person doesn't actually stop and attend to them, for instance, stopping to read the e-mails.

It appears that modern social and academic demands make it nearly impossible for children not to multitask, and although the aforementioned research shows that multitasking is not effective in adults and that poor focus control in children predicts poor life outcomes, there has, until recently, been little research on the impact of electronic multitasking in children.

In a 2005 Kaiser Family Foundation survey, which reported the growth of media multitasking among 8- to 18-year-olds, researchers found that American children were spending 6.5 hours a day on media. Troubling was that in that time, they were spending 8.5 hours' worth of media exposure within those 6.5 hours by using more than one electronic device at a time. Even more concerning was that a 2010 update on the research noted that due to the rapid evolution of electronic devices, the 2005 survey had not asked about smartphones and further noted that due to the fast and ever-evolving digital technology and media, research such as theirs cannot keep pace and as such as soon as results are reported they are outdated.

Harvard psychologist Professor Daniel Goleman has suggested that there are three types of focus: inner, other, and outer. He defines inner focus as the ability to attend to the deepest self, such as what a person would do during mindfulness. Other focus is the ability to zero in on what others are saying, thinking, and feeling by paying attention to their words as well as attending to their nonverbal signals, such as facial expressions and body language. Outer focus is the ability to discern what is going on in the world at large and then integrating the relevant information into a person's experience. When a person is distracted from paying attention by incoming electronic and other stimuli, there is a disruption in the person's ability to use all of these focus demands effectively.

In recent years brain-boosting devices have been all the rage at trade shows. They claim to improve all sorts of brain functions such as the ability to fight fatigue, to focus harder, to block distractions, and to relax. Their promoters further state that they have the research to back them up; however, many of the studies have been done by the companies themselves or by researchers invested in the companies. Jared Horvath, a cognitive neuroscientist at the University of Melbourne in Australia, has said that the only way for the claim that electronic mind-stimulation techniques could help in sport to be taken seriously is to do independent studies. He focused his research on the effects on sports performance and reviewed more than 400 research papers on the matter and published his findings (2015). He found no evidence that the devices worked. The irony is that the very thing that athletes and others are trying to target, the improvement of focus, is best done through the practice of mindfulness, which is free rather than the use of pricey electronics.

There are clearly many benefits to modern electronic media; however, the research is clear that it is changing our brains and that, for now, these devices do not have the power that mindfulness meditation has in training the essential attentional circuits fundamental for self-awareness, academics, and relationships.

34. What is the impact of social media on mindfulness?

Research is clear that the connections that social media bring can be enriching, enhance communication skills, increase creativity and knowledge acquisition, and improve technical proficiency. However, the instant nature of social media also means that as soon as persons connect, they are bombarded by information that is likely to cause a, at times, powerful emotional experience. Seeing injustice may cause anger; hearing about loss may lead to sadness; social media may also cause a new romantic relationship of a friend, jealousy, or happiness. In many cases it is nearly impossible to not have any emotional reaction at all. Recent news stories and research have shown other potential problems, ones that can cause significant mental health problems, associated with excessive social media usage. These include cyber-bullying, addiction to social media, and sexual harassment.

Research associate Maeve Duggan at the Pew Research Center published in 2014 reported that over the past decade almost three-quarters of adult Internet users (73%) now use at least one social media site and 42 percent use multiple social media sites. Further research also shows that about 50 percent of adolescents use social media sites more than once per day, and nearly a quarter of all teens log on to social media sites more than 10 times per day.

The brain is wired to judge and to compare, and in comparisons it is inevitable that people compare themselves to others, particularly their friends. Countless research studies have shown that comparative thinking plays an important role in how persons see themselves in comparison to self and in comparison to their broader social network.

The underlying brain networks involved in social comparison shows that connections between the brain's parietal and frontal lobes are key. These networks are particularly important when comparing levels of attractiveness, height, and social status. Before social media, the number of others persons could compare themselves to was limited by the number of people in their social network and their access to print media. Today, not only is the number of people and connections nearly limitless, but editing tools mean that images can be curated in such a way that the lives of others can seem unattainable.

In adolescence, the brain is hardwired for self-consciousness. The reason is likely evolutionary, in that being aware of how we come across will impact mate selection. The downside in an era of social media is that adolescents are unhappier and more narcissistic.

Social rewards and punishments feel the same whether they come in person or online. The reward chemical dopamine is released when we are praised and we feel pain when we are rejected, whether it happens online or off. Again, because of the volume of social media interactions, the chances of either reward or punishment happening are in direct proportion to the amount of time a person stays online.

Social media is here to stay, and simply producing evidence that its overuse is damaging to young minds will not prevent young people from going online. The data that it can significantly impact brains in an adverse way is balanced by the fact that it is a way in which many people, and in particular young people, do connect. The task then is to find a way to bring mindfulness to the connected masses.

Although there is presently no research on mindful social media, Psychologist Dr. Christopher Willard (2016), a recognized expert and author in the clinical application of mindfulness, has proposed a social media mindfulness practice for exploring favorite sites and their impact on the individual.

The practice includes the standard posture where a person sits in a comfortable yet alert position and then uses the breath to anchor the self in the present moment. Once settled, the task is to then turn on the smartphone, tablet, or computer.

The next task is to reflect on intentions and expectations and, then while focusing on the social media icons, to notice physical sensations, emotions, and thoughts. The next step is to focus on these sensations and experiences with eyes closed while taking purposeful breaths. Then, with open eyes the meditator looks at the first update status or photo and then closes his or her eyes once again and notices his or her emotional, cognitive, and physical responses and then does this for sessions lasting three to five minutes.

The idea is that by noticing the way that social media makes a person feel, he or she can experience a mindful approach to engaging with it. This in turn will allow the practitioner to make better decisions about how often, or whether, to visit the sites. This practice, in turn, underscores the idea that mindfulness can be practiced under many circumstances and using the technologies of the time.

35. Can apps help someone be mindful?

Back in the day when our evolutionary predecessors were hunting mastodons, or pioneers were setting out in wagons to establish new lives in the West, focus and attention were essential in order to survive. Loss of focus could mean the loss of a meal or being attacked by some hungry predator. And yet in those days, distractions were comparatively few and it was easier to pay attention to the task at hand. Fast-forward to today when we are bombarded by a constant influx of information and activity that grab our attention.

Being forced to pay attention to all the noise around us is a main contributor to becoming stressed out. A major source of the fast-flowing information is the advent of technologies that keep us connected to all aspects of the world around us. Much of this technology has meant that our lives are more productive. We can listen to music, take in a sports game, send an e-mail, deposit a check, go grocery shopping, and book a plane ticket without having to move from the couch. And yet this increase in productivity means that the expectation to do more increases. Because of this, technology is not typically considered to be a tool for mindfulness. Our smartphones and tablets have become so seemingly essential that the idea of being without them for even a day can lead to anxiety. The fact that technology can tell us where to go and how to get there, find articles that would have required a trip to a library, and help play games with others and without having to get up off the couch means having to think less and in turn more mindlessness. And yet the fire that can burn our house down is also the fire that can cook our food.

And so if technology can have such adverse effects and steer us to mindlessness, can they help us be mindful? The irony is that it is not the fault of the technology. A smartphone sitting quietly on a kitchen counter is not a problem. Rather, it is the unrelenting reliance and use of the smartphone that hijacks our capacity for mindfulness. Technology will permeate all of our lives. We will not undo all advances to hunt mastodons. Mindfulness is less about disconnecting from the modern technological world and more about making a choice to pay attention in spite of it, and perhaps even using some aspects of technology as a guide to becoming more aware.

One way to do this is through the use of a software application more commonly known as an "app." In reviewing various mindfulness apps, most guide the listener to a mindful practice in a way that is consistent with effective practice and could be a first step toward a practice less reliant on the app. Any app that is going to be effective should have the following qualities:

A guide that instructs the listener to pay attention to physical experiences: This includes attending to your heart and breathing rate, noticing the tension in your various muscle groups, and noticing pain or discomfort. In some circumstances having a blood pressure machine may be helpful and having the app remind you to get a physical exam, including blood work that tests sugar and cholesterol levels, can help establish a baseline of health. This baseline can be used as a reference point from which to compare the impact of mindfulness on overall health status.

A tracking ability to monitor certain activities: Exercise, sleep, and food intake all impact state of mind and wellness. Unfettered access to highly refined, high-calorie foods means that mindlessness has led to an unprecedented rate of obesity throughout the world, and it is particularly bad in the United States. An effective app can help track how many calories you consume and burn, and then wearable devices can interface with the app to monitor sleep quality, activity level, and heart rate. Paying mindful attention to these data allows you to make a choice about continuing or changing your behavior.

A mechanism by which meaningful connections are strengthened: Zen master and teacher Thich Nhat Hanh once said: "The most precious gift we can offer others is our presence. When mindfulness embraces those we love, they will bloom like flowers." Constant connectivity has meant a connectivity of sorts. Increasingly, the amount of time we spend together is not a physical, in-person connection, and this can mean that communication does not take place in real time.

Facial expressions, tone of voice, and an ability to explore intentions can be lost. If the app can direct the user to connect in person, even if it is simply the act of making a phone or video call to a loved one, then the app is fostering mindfulness of relationship.

Elicit awareness of responses to the stress brought on by technology: The app should encourage disconnection from technology in order to allow users to recognize the impact of technology on their mind, body, behavior, and habitual responses. It should encourage the noticing of thought patterns in the absence of technology. Is there a withdrawal experience? Does the fear of missing out on what is happening in the connected world arise? Observing automatic, often mindless, reactions to the way the mind and body respond to the presence or absence of technology can be a powerful way to take back control of emotional, relational, and behavioral responses.

There is some research on the use of such apps. For instance, a study by Annika Howells in 2014 explored the viability of delivering a positive psychological intervention in app format to people seeking happiness. The study randomly assigned participants to participate in either an empirically supported mindfulness intervention ($n = 57$) or a control intervention ($n = 64$) for 10 days. A control intervention is one in which the result is not intended to elicit mindfulness. The study explored smartphone methodology, the importance of empirically based content for well-being enhancement, and the extent to which user experience related to well-being gains.

The results showed significant increases in positive mood states and a reduction in depression in the mindfulness group. There were no such gains in the control group. The authors concluded that smartphone-based mindfulness interventions not only were viable but could significantly enhance elements of well-being.

On the other hand, a more extensive review by Madhavan Mani of Australia's Institute of Health and Biomedical Innovation in 2015 evaluated mindfulness-based iPhone apps and concluded that although many apps claim to be mindfulness related, most were simply guided meditation apps, timers, or reminders. Very few had high ratings on the Mobile Application Rating Scale, and on the whole there was presently little available evidence on just how effective such apps are in helping the practitioner using the app develop mindfulness.

It is too early to tell whether apps will help in the pursuit of a mindful practice. The truest of tests as to their utility in getting the practitioner to be mindful will be the ability to so practice whether or not the app is available and ultimately to be able to discard the app altogether.

---·❖·---

Case Studies

MARIA

Maria is a 42-year-old who recently moved to Boston from Los Angeles. Ever since going through a complicated divorce involving many lawyers and court appearances, she has experienced bouts of depression and symptoms of anxiety. She could not let go of the fact that her ex had been cheating on her and to make it worse had being doing so with her half-sister.

After the divorce, she did four years of psychoanalysis and took medication but felt no better. She felt that by leaving Los Angeles and moving to Boston she could get away from her problems. Instead, Maria fell into a state of depression; she had trouble falling asleep and then woke up frequently through the night, ruminating on all that had happened. The little sleep that she did have was filled with nightmares of having been abused as a child by a family friend. She lost her appetite and didn't want to spend time with even her closest friends.

When she got to Boston she went to see a psychiatrist, who prescribed her a different antidepressant medication, but she developed side effects and felt more anxious. Eventually her work as a creative director at her advertising firm started to suffer. She could not shake the memories of the divorce. As her creative output diminished, she started to worry she would be fired and so requested a medical leave.

While waiting for a medical appointment in her doctor's waiting room, she had read a magazine article on mindfulness as a way to treat various conditions, including mental illness. The article was on mindfulness-based cognitive therapy (MBCT), an approach specifically designed to help people who suffer from depression and enduring unhappiness.

After her appointment she went to the website http://mbct.com/ and found more about the treatment and how to find a therapist. She scheduled an appointment and told the MBCT therapist that neither four years of medication nor traditional therapy had helped lessen her depression. She admitted that she was somewhat hopeless and skeptical that anything would work.

Her therapist explained that MBCT combined elements of cognitive therapy with the meditative practices of mindfulness. "What this treatment will do is to get you to recognize that you can see your symptoms in a new way, and by doing so, and then be able to behave in a new way, one that is more compatible and consistent with a life of joy."

After an explanation of the treatment, Maria joined a group of other people who similarly struggled with depression and anxiety. At the initial session, her therapist told her that her anxiety was causing her to have distracting and recurring thoughts that had taken too much control over her overall experience. The therapist continued: "These are unproductive worries and you can train your mind to see your situation completely differently. And it is these thoughts that lead to depression. When you become aware of the thoughts through the practice of mindfulness, you say to yourself: 'There goes my mind again. I've been here before. It is just a thought, one about the past and not something happening now.'"

Over the next few months Maria began to understand her depression and to notice the situations in her life that made her vulnerable to downward mood spirals. She began to recognize the things that got her stuck at the bottom of her spiral as well as the things that made her feel better. She realized that the low moods were connected to thoughts of feeling worthless and that in those moments she lost touch with the activities and relationships that made her life worth living. Through observation, her body sensations, urges to isolate from life, and thoughts associated with depression, Maria became more aware and mindful of both the positive and negative experiences linked to her depression. For example, when she noticed depression setting in, she also noticed old responses—like isolating from friends—coming into her mind. Noticing the responses in turn allowed her to change she felt by altering the old habitual reactions. She was no longer unaware of what had influenced her moods. Over time her mood started to lift, and she found a more fulfilling and less anxiety and depressed life in her adopted city.

Analysis

The onset of Maria's depressive episodes was specific to her situation and, in particular, her divorce. This type of event-triggered onset is common with recurrent depression. Her sense of hopelessness came from the belief that she did not expect anything to make her feel better given her past experience with medication and therapy. Her isolation from friends and pleasurable activities prevented her from having positive experiences in her life. Her history of childhood abuse could have explained her nonresponse to medication as research shows that trauma victims tend not to response as well as nonvictims to medication.

The group therapy provided her a community of other people similarly suffering from depression. It offered her hope that, like the others, she could develop the mindfulness skills that would allow her to better control her moods. Her daily homework meant that she was doing therapy every day, which forced her to focus on mindfulness. Part of the homework included a technique called the three-minute breathing space. This encouraged her to include formal mindfulness practice into her typical day. As her understanding of depression grew and her practice in mindfulness became routine, she noted an increase in her control over her mood. Over the eight weeks of the treatment Maria noted an improved ability to concentrate, not only on therapy but on all aspects of her life. Ultimately, her depression improved to the point that she could manage without the need for medication.

Maria also understood that although most people feel sad at some point in their lives, what she experienced, clinical depression is a mental disorder marked by the symptoms she experienced. At its worst, people with depression can have suicidal thoughts and suicidal behavior. By finally finding a treatment that worked for her, her condition never reached those depths.

FELICITY

Felicity is a 20-year-old junior at college, who has steadily gained weight since her freshman year. Some months ago, her primary care physician told her that she needed to lose 50 pounds. Despite countless diets, diet pills, and periodic visits to the gym, her weight continued to go up. She admits that she has not been consistent with any of the suggested approaches, but now her weight gain is affecting her relationships and she worries that she will never get a boyfriend unless she slims down.

Felicity has been told over and over that she has to eat less, eat healthier, and exercise more. The problem she noted is that diets are hard to keep to and the medications make her jittery or give her other side effects. When she had the jittery side effect, she could not sleep, and she had gone to a walk-in clinic where she was given a prescription medication. She noted that the medication made her very hungry and eventually she went back to her primary care physician.

When Felicity had first been evaluated by her primary care physician, he did all kinds of tests, but she has come to accept that there is no obvious medical condition to explain her weight gain. Genetics work against her as there is some obesity on her mother's side of the family. This time she wants it to be different. She has made a serious commitment to herself and to lose weight and heard from one of her roommates that mindfulness may be an alternative solution.

Felicity was referred by her primary care physician to a mindfulness-based eating awareness training (MB-EAT) program. Like other contemporary mindfulness interventions, MB-EAT was modeled after Kabat-Zinn's mindfulness-based stress reduction (MBSR). Specifically, the treatment has 12 dedicated group sessions and assigned homework.

Felicity's mindfulness focus was to learn tune into her natural physical hunger signals at every moment. What was her body telling her? How strong was her hunger? Was there a trigger to eat a particular food? What were her emotions at the time of eating?

Once Felicity decided to eat, she was taught how mindful eating involved really tasting her food. Research shows that after a few bites taste buds become dull to the food. She started to ask herself: "Why do I keep eating if I can't taste the food as much? And am I still getting pleasure from the food?" She learned to tell when she had had enough food and that it takes time for the digestion to send nutrients to the brain so that even though she might still feel hungry after a meal, waiting a while to digest the food would allow the message to get to the brain before eating more.

Felicity learned to choose foods differently. For instance, she loved chocolate. She could get a large bar of chocolate for the same amount of money that she could a smaller gourmet chocolate. She changed quantity for quality, enjoying the smaller yet more delicious chocolate over the larger quantity. She used 2 percent milk in her cereal over full cream milk and noticed that it did not change the taste too much.

And finally Felicity learned that like all mindfulness practices, mindful eating involved becoming more mindful, and soon she was using mindfulness practices in other aspects of her life beyond eating.

As Felicity worked through the exercises in the group program, she noted several shifts occurring. Her mindfulness practice helped her to relax. She began to notice how judgmental she was toward herself and other people in her life and, in particular, that she was a failure. She noticed how she would eat past the point of feeling full and that with this came the thought that she was being deprived of something that other people could have.

As Felicity became more relaxed at college, her tendency to order pizza late at night, after a full dinner, ended. She allowed herself to eat and enjoy some of her roommates' treats; however, she was able to stop after a single serving. She also became more aware of hunger and fullness and noticed that she could adjust her meal sizes to smaller portions and then wait because she would feel full and not have to continue eating. She ordered smaller sizes from takeout so that there would be no temptation to raid the refrigerator late at night. She stopped eating in front of the television and ate before going to the movies so that she would not load up on buttery popcorn during the show.

The changes in Felicity's behavior took time and did not happen overnight. This is because long-standing patterns take time to change. Her mindfulness techniques gave her the tools to continue to notice the patterns that had become so habitual. Over the following year, she found that her mindful eating became easier and she steadily lost weight. As she became more confident in herself, she felt more in control of her life and then smiled to herself one day when a young man awkwardly asked for her number after class. She knew just how far she had come.

Analysis

Felicity is not alone in her struggle. The most recent U.S. data shows that 70.7 percent of adults over the age of 20 are either overweight or clinically obese. The most common cause is one of basic math. She struggled with a negative energy balance, and this is what at most often causes obesity. Energy balance occurs when the energy that persons put into their body equals the energy they use. This energy comes from the calories provided by food and drinks. Energy out is the amount of energy the body uses to stay alive, like lungs breathing, heart beating, brain thinking, and gut digesting food as well as the energy used to be physically active.

In order to lose weight, energy going out must be more than energy coming in. For Felicity, a negative energy balance meant that the energy she was ingesting was greater than the energy she was using and so she put on weight.

The mindfulness approach helped Felicity notice things that could make a difference, such as spending too little time outside and too much time lying around on the couch watching reruns of her favorite crime show on TV. She also noted the over-sized portions at fast-food restaurants and that often these came with a lack of healthy food choices. At night she noted how carbohydrate cravings made her susceptible to TV advertising encouraging high-calorie foods.

Although there was nothing Felicity could do about her genetic profile, staying away from high-calorie, fatty foods meant that she reduced the impact of her genetics. She was also careful about noting whether medications caused weight gain or not. She also learned about the impact of stress and poor sleep on weight gain and through mindful practice was able to reduce stress and get better sleep at night. All of these factors added up to a healthier, and lighter, life experience.

JOSEPH

Joseph is a 61-year-old executive at a multinational company, who has been experiencing significant stress at work. He was on the verge of signing some big deals, but none had yet materialized. This meant many corporate meetings with big lunches and even bigger dinners. His weight ballooned, and he was struggling to get his gym. He increased his smoking to a pack a day, saying it was the only thing that calmed his nerves. His annual checkup revealed very high cholesterol levels, and his doctor warned him that he was putting himself at great risk.

After a heart attack his boss told him that he had to take a vacation, but he refused to do so. He was terrified that he would lose his job if he took time off to recuperate. And with the fear of losing his job came the thought that he would not be able to provide for his family. He told his doctor that he was certain that he "would be replaced by one of the young and ambitious managers" on his team.

Rather than take a vacation, he followed his doctor's other advice and started to lose some weight and had cut back on his smoking to five cigarettes a day. He had wanted to exercise more, but his work schedule had him exhausted by the time he came home, and then he found it difficult to get up early to go to the gym before work. After the heart attack, he was referred to a cardiologist.

Joseph told her that he felt insecure and anxious. He acknowledged that he had gone back to work soon after being in hospital and he found himself making minor mistakes at work and feared being caught out. He started to compare himself to his peers and felt that he was a personal and professional failure. Despite being encouraged to take a rest by the human resources department, he remained reluctant to ask the company president for some time off. The cardiologist recommended a course of mindfulness-based stress reduction (MBSR). She told him, "It will help you deal with your anxiety and your fears. It will also help in addressing your stress."

For Joseph, a lifestyle of unrelenting work, eating without exercising, stress, and anxiety took its toll on his heart. His reason for applying mindfulness in the form of MBSR was pragmatic; he did not want to have another heart attack. He joined a group with 15 other executives and committed to an eight-week program. He practiced meditation, yoga postures, and mindfulness during stressful situations and social interactions and then did 45 minutes of homework each night. Over the eight weeks of the course, be began to notice more peacefulness, better sleep, less fear, more flexibility, and better relationships not only at work but also with his wife and children.

Joseph actively cultivated some of the key attitudes of the mindfulness practice, without compromising his work output. He was less judgmental and more curious while still insisting on accountability. He became less frustrated when things did not go his way and less attached to the outcome and noted that by doing so, he could more quickly let go of disappointment and more quickly move on to problem solving. He became more patient with employees who were struggling and found that by doing so they were more likely to come to him for help and, as such, by taking a little more time with his employees in the moment, he saved a lot more time later on trying to fix mistakes or clear up a mess. Consistent with other scientific findings on mindfulness research, he also experienced a reduction in blood pressure, his weight trended down, and he was better able at leaving his work at work and enjoy his leisure time at home without fretting too much. His fear that he would be laid off lessened when his boss, recognizing his new attitude and productivity, rewarded him with a promotion and bonus.

Analysis

Joseph is hardly alone in his struggle. Heart disease is one of the leading causes of death worldwide. Specifically, coronary artery disease is a condition in which the walls of the blood vessels that supply blood to the heart muscle become narrowed, and eventually totally blocked, by a fatty material called atheroma. This is made worse if the person has a family history of heart illness, is a cigarette smoker, is obese, and has high blood pressure. In addition, factors such as stress, depression, and anxiety increase the chance of heart illness because stress hormones accelerate the formation of the atheroma narrowing.

With the practice of mindfulness he learned to focus his attention on his body rather than the catastrophic thoughts in his mind. This led him to increasing moments of peace of mind and relaxation. His practice of yoga breathing exercises, stretches, and poses both strengthened his core and made him more flexible, all of which was a long way away from just a few months earlier.

STEVEN

Steven is an 18-year-old high school senior about to graduate. He is hooked on social media and technology. He is struggling because he wants to get into a good college and wants to stay connected with his friends. He recognizes that spending time online has pros and cons. On the one hand when he spends too much time online, he is able to stay in constant contact with friends, but on the other hand he spends less time studying and his grades have been falling. He fears missing out with what everyone is doing, and he knows that if he doesn't study he won't get into the colleges he is interested in attending.

For Steven, the stress of balancing all of these things has had a clear impact on his life. For one thing he is sleeping only about seven hours per night much less than he knows he needs, and he is exhausted the next day. Although part of the poor sleep is staying up late doing homework, a large part is also the constant distraction of texts, Facebook messages, and Snapchats. His poor sleep in turn led to the cycle of more stress, more anxiety about doing everything, and less good-quality sleep. Then, and although he was on his cross-country team, in recent months he had been attending fewer practices and getting less exercise. His eating habits had become poor, and so while he had been at his fitness during training and meets he had made sure to eat three balanced meals a day; now he was skipping meals and then relying on coffee and sugary foods for nutrition and energy.

Steven had heard of mindfulness and knew that there was an after-school group that met twice a week for two hours each time. He had read that his favorite basketball player, Kobe Bryant, practiced mindfulness and that Steve Jobs, the founder of Apple, had used it as well. When his cross-country coach mentioned it and his wellness teacher said that mindfulness could reduce stress, improve memory, improve relationships, and, most important, improve test scores, he decided he would join the group.

Steven committed to an eight-week course that focused on mindful awareness practices for students. He changed his relationship with his smartphone; for instance, instead of using it to listen to music, he used a guided meditation app to focus on the sound of a bell. He learned about mindful eating and ways to rest his mind from the thousands of worry thoughts that plagued him each night before he went to bed. Over the eight weeks he noticed that he became less stressed and was less emotional. He noticed reduced worry when he felt that he wouldn't complete an assignment on time. He was able to concentrate for longer periods of time on homework without being distracted by the TV or his social media. Although he wasn't sure how his end-of-term exams would turn out, he felt more confident and was certain that because he was less stressed and less distracted, he could say that he had given his priorities his full attention.

Steven's main reason for enrolling in the mindfulness group had been the looming college decision; he had come to the realization that if he could not handle his senior year of high school, there was no way he was ever going to handle freshman year in college. Over the eight weeks of twice-a-week, two-hour mindfulness practice sessions, together with mindfulness homework assigned each time, he began to notice less stress, better sleep, getting back to eating more healthily, and better relationships with his friends and teachers. He understood more of the schoolwork being taught in class and was less distracted, and with this he was completing the assignments more consistently. In turn, his goal of getting into a good college became realistic.

Analysis

Students like Steven understand that they have to do well, particularly in the last two years of school. However, balancing the goal of getting good grades in order to maximize their chance of getting into a good college while participating in team sports, doing after-school activities, doing homework, and being online with friends means that during the school year, high school students are the most stressed group of people in America, according to a 2014 American Psychological Association (APA) survey. The same report found that over the past year only 16 percent of teens reported that their stress decreased, while 31 percent said that their stress had increased.

For Steven, weeks of unrelenting homework, cross-country running, poor eating, and being glued to his social media had led to increased stress, worsening relationships with his teachers, and slipping grades. With regard to sleep, he was getting nearly two hours less than what is recommended for teenagers by the National Sleep Foundation. Finally, his total daily time online was over four hours, and this amount of time is also associated with high levels of stress according to the APA survey, which found that teens who spent an average of more than three hours online per day were far more stressed than those who spent two hours a day or less.

Steven actively brought some of the key attitudes of the mindfulness practice to his relationships and his work. By spending more face-to-face time with his friends, he found that he could listen and see that they too were stressed, that his fear that he was missing out on parties was a misguided one, and that many of his friends were similarly worried about their senior year; he recognized that the glamorous postings on social media did not also capture the negative scenes of the police showing up and friends ending up in hospital with alcohol poisoning. By paying better attention in class, he learned and understood more, and he found that he did better on quizzes without having to study more. He became less frustrated in the moments when he didn't understand things and was more likely to approach his teachers for help. Because they saw how hard he was trying, they, in turn, were less likely to see him as "goofing off" and welcomed his questions. He noticed a reduction in the two fears that had paralyzed him, first his fear that he would not make it to college or that if he did that he would fail and second his fear of being disconnected from his friends. With his increase in mindfulness practice, he noticed an increase in inner peace and felt in far more control of his life.

MARY

Mary is a 30-year-old doctoral student in psychology who feels unfulfilled in her life and is looking for a new direction. She has noticed what she calls "a spiritual void" and is unsettled by the idea that "this is it; all we do is live and then die and put up with all the stuff in between." She feels a hunger for spirituality without the need to belong to a faith, one that is going to "dictate her beliefs, morals and practices." She does not like the idea that there is nothing more to life than simple existence. She is not depressed or anxious and does not feel that she needs either a therapist or a priest to find meaning. After reading an article on mindfulness in the *Huffington Post*, she decided that it might provide some answers and decided to explore the practice further.

In the article Mary read that taking in the glory of nature from the top of a mountain peak, standing back and noticing the beauty of a piece of art, or throwing herself fully into a hymn of worship were all experiences that lead to a sense of awe or experience of amazement of fascination that persons feel when they encounter something larger than themselves. The article explained that when awe is experienced in a moment, it turns these moments into a powerfully protective mechanism when it comes to physical and mental health. Mary wanted to be able to experience such awe in her life and joined a meditation group at her local Zen center. Over time she met people from all social, ethnic, political, and religious walks of life and understood that they had different reasons for being there.

With her Zen teacher she learned to sit with stillness and that this stillness connected her with her inner self. Through this particular practice of mindfulness, she began to cultivate the experience of awe, because, as she noticed, the stillness of meditation set the conditions for her to begin to experience moments of awe. Distractions in her everyday life had prevented this from happening before.

As Mary continued to practice on a regular basis, she noted a feeling of increasing connectedness that she had not felt in a long time. By paying mindful attention to everyday life moments, she recognized that she could no longer easily define the complexities of life. Things were far more nuanced, and there were no words to express the magnitude of the joy or the experience she noted when taking in the views from the top of a mountain after a long hike or when looking out the window of her office on the seventh floor of her building down to the street below. Her brain began to change as she accommodated and contemplated the vastness of how even simple things are. She began seeing all things as what they were not only in their immediate context of their surroundings but also their place on the planet, the planet's place in the galaxy, and the galaxy's place in the universe. With all of this she discovered a spiritual stillness and peace that had eluded her for a long time and then realized her life to be far less meaningless that she had thought it to be.

Analysis

For Mary, dissatisfaction with formal religious practice left her facing a meaningless life, which in turn did not appeal to her. Although she did not necessarily believe in God, she also did not believe that this world was all there was.

Although there are many people who practice their faith in a traditional way, many others are dissatisfied with the orthodoxy of defined religions. This is borne out by research which shows that the share of Americans who consider themselves Christian is falling fast, while the number of people considering themselves atheist, agnostic, and "nothing in particulars" continues to grow. Despite this, and even though many Americans like Mary are religiously unaffiliated, most consider their spiritual life to be important in their lives; and even though she did not have a dedicated therapist, by connecting with a spiritual leader in a spiritual community she was able to fill the void of meaning she had experienced.

Glossary

Beginner's mind: A mind that is open and curious to the experience of the moment as if being experienced for the first time.

Buddha: A fully awakened person, specifically the historical Buddha who lived and taught in India 2,500 years ago.

Dana or *daana*: The concept of giving generously without expecting any form of repayment from the recipient.

Dharma: The teachings of the Buddha.

Ego: The pattern of conditioned habits that a person mistakens for a sense of self.

Emptiness: A term applied to the recognition that things do not arise independently and further that things are interconnected and therefore empty of independent existence.

Enlightenment: Awakening.

Four Noble Truths: The core of the Buddhist teaching reflecting on the nature of and then the ending of suffering.

Meditation retreat: Typically a secluded place where a person can set aside a period of time for the development of wisdom and compassion through sustained mindfulness meditation practice.

Metta: Loving kindness meditation used to cultivate a capacity for an open and loving heart. The practice leads to the development of fearlessness, happiness, and a greater capacity to love.

Mindfulness-based stress reduction (MBSR): A secular mindfulness-based training for reducing stress and pain associated with chronic medical illnesses, developed by Jon Kabat-Zinn.

Pali: The language in which the teachings of the Buddha were recorded.

Sangha: A community of practitioners of the Buddhist path.

Vipassana: Insight meditation or the practice of moment-to-moment mindfulness with the goal of developing a calm awareness into the nature of experience, in turn leading to wisdom, compassion, and the end of suffering.

Yoga: A system of spiritual development incorporating the practice of specific physical postures, breathing exercises, and meditation.

Yogi: A person undertaking the spiritual path of awakening.

Zen: A meditative form of Buddhist practice that evolved in China and then spread to Japan and Korea.

Directory of Resources

BOOKS AND ARTICLES

Albrecht, N. J. (2015). *Teachers teaching mindfulness with children* (Doctoral thesis, Flinders University, South Australia).

Bishop, S. R., Lau, M., Shapiro, S., Carlson, L., Anderson, N. D., Carmody, J., . . . Devins, G. (2004). "Mindfulness: A proposed operational definition." *Clinical Psychology: Science and Practice, 11*, 230–241.

Bowen, S., Witkiewitz, K., Clifasefi, S. L., Grow, J., Chawla, N., . . . Larimer, M. E. (2014). Relative efficacy of mindfulness-based relapse prevention, standard relapse prevention, and treatment as usual for substance use disorders: A randomized clinical trial. *JAMA Psychiatry, 71*(5), 547–556.

Brand, S., Holsboer-Trachsler, E., Naranjo, J. R., & Schmidt, S. (2012). Influence of mindfulness practice on cortisol and sleep in long-term and short-term meditators. *Neuropsychobiology, 3*, 109–118.

Carlson, L. E., Speca, M., Faris, P., & Patel, K. D. (2007). One year pre-post intervention follow-up of psychological, immune, endocrine and blood pressure outcomes of mindfulness-based stress reduction (MBSR) in breast and prostate cancer outpatients. *Brain, Behavior, and Immunity, 21*(8), 1038–1049.

Cassady, J. C., & Johnson, R. E. (2002). Cognitive test anxiety and academic performance. *Contemporary Educational Psychology, 27*(2), 270.

Creswell, J. D., Myers, H. F., Cole, S. W., & Irwin, M. R. (2009). Mindfulness meditation training effects on CD4+ T lymphocytes in HIV-1 infected adults: A small randomized controlled trial. *Brain, Behavior, and Immunity, 23*(2), 184–188.

Curtin, S. C., Warner, M., & Hedegaard, H. (2016). Increase in suicide in the United States, 1999–2014. NCHS Data Brief No. 241. Hyattsville, MD: National Center for Health Statistics.

Djokovic, N. (2013). *Serve to win.* New York, NY: Random House.

Duggan, M., & Smith, A. (2014) *Social media update 2013.* Washington, DC: Pew Research Center.

Eisendrath, S. J., Gillung, E., Hartzler, A., James-Myers, M., Wolkowitz, O., Sipe, W., . . . Delucchi, K. (2016). Mindfulness-based cognitive therapy associated with decreases in C-reactive protein in major depressive disorder: A pilot study. *Journal of Alternative, Complementary and Integrative Medicine, 2*(10).

Feliu-Soler, A., Pascual, J. C., Borràs, X., Portella, M. J., Martín-Blanco, A., Armario, A., . . . Soler, J. (2014). Effects of dialectical behaviour therapy-mindfulness training on emotional reactivity in borderline personality disorder: Preliminary results. *Clinical Psychology & Psychotherapy, 21*(4), 363–370.

Fischer, R. (1971). A cartography of the ecstatic and meditative states. *Science, 174*(4012), 897–904.

Fontanella, C. A., Hiance-Steelesmith, D. L., Phillips, G. S., Bridge, J. A., Lester, N., Sweeney, H. A., & Campo, J. V. (2015). Widening rural-urban disparities in youth suicides, United States, 1996–2010. *JAMA Pediatrics, 169*(5), 466–473.

Gallagher, R. P. (2014). *National survey of college counseling centers.* The American College Counseling Association, 1, 55.

Gardner, F. L., & Moore, Z. E. (2001, October). The multi-level classification system for sport psychology (MCS-SP): Toward a structured assessment and conceptualization of athlete-clients. Workshop presented at the Annual Conference of the Association for the Advancement of Applied Sport Psychology, Orlando, Florida.

Gardner, F. L., & Moore, Z. E. (2012). Mindfulness and acceptance models in sport psychology: A decade of basic and applied scientific advancements. *Canadian Psychology/Psychologie Canadienne, 53*(4), 309.

Grof, C., & Grof, S. (1992). *Stormy search for the self.* New York, NY: Jeremy P. Tarcher.

Grossman, P., Niemann, L., Schmidt, S., & Walach, H. (2004). Mindfulness-based stress reduction and health benefits. A meta-analysis. *Journal of Psychosomatic Research, 57,* 35–43.

Grossman, P., Tiefenthaler-Gilmer, U., Raysz, A., & Kesper, U. (2007). Mindfulness training as an intervention for fibromyalgia: Evidence of postintervention and 3-year follow-up benefits in well-being. *Psychotherapy and Psychosomatics, 76*(4), 226–233.

Grow, Kory. (2015, November 5). Katy Perry, Sting Stun at David Lynch's Meditation Benefit Concert. Retrieved from http://www.rollingstone.com/music/news/katy-perry-sting-stun-at-david-lynchs-meditation-benefit-concert-20151105

Hasenkamp, W., & Barsalou, L. W. (2012). Effects of meditation experience on functional connectivity of distributed brain networks. *Frontiers in Human Neuroscience, 6*, 1–14.

Heffner, K. L., Crean, H. F., & Kemp, J. E. (2016). Meditation programs for veterans with posttraumatic stress disorder: Aggregate findings from a multi-site evaluation. *Psychological Trauma: Theory, Research, Practice, and Policy, 8*(3), 365.

Herron, R. E., & Cavanaugh, K. (2005). Can the transcendental meditation program reduce the medical expenditures of older people? A longitudinal cost reduction study in Canada. *Journal of Social Behavior and Personality, 17*, 415–442.

Hofmann, A. (1979/2009). *LSD, my problem child: Reflections on sacred drugs, mysticism, and science.* Sarasota, FL: Multidisciplinary Association for Psychedelic Studies.

Hölzel, B. K., Brunsch, V., Gard, T., Greve, D. N., Koch, K., Sorg, C., . . . Milad, M. R. (2016). Mindfulness-based stress reduction, fear conditioning, and the uncinate fasciculus: A pilot study. *Frontiers in Behavioral Neuroscience, 10*.

Horvath, J. C., Forte, J. D., & Carter, O. (2015). Quantitative review finds no evidence of cognitive effects in healthy populations from single-session transcranial direct current stimulation (tDCS). *Brain Stimulation, 8*(3), 535–550.

Howells, A., Ivtzan, I., & Eiroa-Orosa, F. J. (2014). Putting the "app" in happiness: A randomised controlled trial of a smartphone-based mindfulness intervention to enhance wellbeing. *Journal of Happiness Studies,* 1–23.

Huffington, Arianna. (2014). *Thrive: The third metric to redefining success and creating a life of well-being, wisdom, and wonder.* New York, NY: Harmony.

Hülsheger, U. R., Alberts, H. J. E. M., Feinholdt, A., & Lang, J. W. B. (2013). Benefits of mindfulness at work: The role of mindfulness in emotion regulation, emotional exhaustion, and job satisfaction. *Journal of Applied Psychology, 98*(2), 310–325.

Hülsheger, U. R., Lang, J., Alberts, H., Depenbrock, F., Fehrman, C., & Zijlstra, F. R. H. (2014). The power of presence: The role of mindfulness at work for daily levels and change trajectories of psychological detachment and sleep quality. *Journal of Applied Psychology*, 99(6), 1113–1128.

Kabat-Zinn, J. (1994). *Wherever you go, there you are: Mindfulness meditation in everyday life*. New York, NY: Hyperion.

Kandel, E. R. (2007). *In search of memory: The emergence of a new science of mind*. New York, NY: WW Norton & Company.

Kant, Immanuel. (1784, September 30). An answer to the question: "What is Enlightenment?" Konigsberg, Prussia. Retrieved from http://library.standrews-de.org/lists/CourseGuides/religion/rs-vi/oppressed/kant_what_is_enlightenment.pdf

Kaufman, K. A., & Glass, C. R. (2006). *Mindful sport performance enhancement: A treatment manual for archers and golfers* (Unpublished manuscript). The Catholic University of America, Washington, DC.

Kristeller, J. L., & Hallett, C. B. (1999). An exploratory study of a meditation-based intervention for binge eating disorder. *Journal of Health Psychology*, 4(3), 357–363.

Kristeller, J. L., & Wolever, R. Q. (2011). Mindfulness-Based Eating Awareness Training for treating binge eating disorder: The conceptual foundation. *Eating Disorders*, 19(1), 49–61.

Kuyken, W., Warren, F. C., Taylor, R. S., Whalley, B., Crane, C., Bondolfi, G., . . . Segal, Z. (2016, June 1). Efficacy of mindfulness-based cognitive therapy in prevention of depressive relapse: An individual patient data meta-analysis from randomized trials. *JAMA Psychiatry*, 73(6), 565–574.

Linehan, M. M. (1993). *Cognitive-behavioral treatment of borderline personality disorder*. New York, NY: The Guilford Press.

Lipschitz, D. L., Kuhn, R., Kinney, A. Y., Donaldson, G. W., & Nakamura, Y. (2013). Reduction in salivary α-amylase levels following a mind–body intervention in cancer survivors—An exploratory study. *Psychoneuroendocrinology*, 38(9), 1521–1531.

Ljótsson, B., Andersson, G., Andersson, E., Hedman, E., Lindfors, P., Andréewitch, S., . . . Lindefors, N. (2011). Acceptability, effectiveness, and cost-effectiveness of internet-based exposure treatment for irritable bowel syndrome in a clinical sample: A randomized controlled trial. *BMC Gastroenterology*, 11(1): 110.

Mani, M., Kavanagh, D. J., Hides, L., & Stoyanov, S. R. (2015). Review and evaluation of mindfulness-based iPhone apps. *JMIR mHealth and uHealth*, 3(3).

Mark, G., Gonzalez, V. M., & Harris, J. (2005, April). No task left behind?: Examining the nature of fragmented work. *Proceedings of the SIGCHI*

Conference on Human Factors in Computing Systems (pp. 321–330). Association for Computing Machinery, New York, NY.

Matchim, Y., Armer, J. M., & Stewart, B. R. (2011, March). Mindfulness-based stress reduction among breast cancer survivors: A literature review and discussion. *Oncology Nursing Forum, 38*(2), E61–E71.

McCracken, L. M., Vowles, K. E., & Eccleston, C. (2005). Acceptance-based treatment for persons with complex, long standing chronic pain: A preliminary analysis of treatment outcome in comparison to a waiting phase. *Behaviour Research and Therapy, 43*(10), 1335–1346.

Miller, C. K., Kristeller, J. L., Headings, A., Nagaraja, H., & Miser, W. F. (2012). Comparative effectiveness of a mindful eating intervention to a diabetes self-management intervention among adults with type 2 diabetes: A pilot study. *Journal of the Academy of Nutrition and Dietetics, 112*(11), 1835–1842.

Moffitt, T. E., Poulton, R., & Caspi, A. (2013). Lifelong impact of early self-control. *American Scientist, 101*(5), 352.

Mrazek, M. D., Franklin, M. S., Phillips, D., Baird, B., & Schooler, J. W. (2013). Mindfulness training improves working memory capacity and GRE performance while reducing mind wandering. *Psychological Science, 24*(5), 776–781.

Pradhan, E. K., Baumgarten, M., Langenberg, P., Handwerger, B., Gilpin, A. K., Magyari, T., . . . Berman, B. M. (2007). Effect of mindfulness-based stress reduction in rheumatoid arthritis patients. *Arthritis Care & Research, 57*(7), 1134–1142.

Rose, Ted. (2009, March 12). Mindful drinking (Vajrayana tradition: alcohol-and-Buddhism). Retrieved from http://www.elephantjournal.com/2009/03/mindful-drinking-vajrayana-tradition-alcohol-and-buddhism/

Rosenthal, Norman E. How meditation changed Hugh Jackman's life. Retrieved from http://www.oprah.com/inspiration/How-Meditation-Changed-Hugh-Jackmans-Life

Rosenzweig, S., Reibel, D. K., Greeson, J. M., & Edman, J. S. (2007). Mindfulness-based stress reduction is associated with improved glycemic control in type 2 diabetes mellitus: A pilot study. *Alternative Therapies in Health and Medicine, 13*(5), 36.

Roth, S. (2003). "The Women's Initiative," Steering Committee Report for the Women's Initiative. Duke University.

Rumi, Jalal. (1994). *Teachings of Rumi* (The Masnavi): *The Spiritual Couplets of Jalaludin Rumi*. Idries Shah (Translator). San Jose, CA: Ishk Book Service.

Schonert-Reichl, K. A., Oberle, E., Lawlor, M. S., Abbott, D., Thomson, K., Oberlander, T. F., & Diamond, A. (2015). Enhancing cognitive and social–emotional development through a simple-to-administer mindfulness-based school program for elementary school children: A randomized controlled trial. *Developmental Psychology, 51*(1), 52.

Schumacher-Brunhes, Marie (2012). *Enlightenment Jewish style: The Haskalah Movement in Europe.* Mainz: Leibniz Institute of European History (IEG).

Smith, A. Guzman-Alvarez, A., Westover, T., Keller, S., & Fuller, S. (2012). *Mindful schools program evaluation.* University of California at Davis, Center for Education and Evaluation Services, Davis, CA.

Sullivan, M. J., Wood, L., Terry, J., Brantley, J., Charles, A., McGee, V., . . . Adams, K. (2009). The Support, Education, and Research in Chronic Heart Failure Study (SEARCH): A mindfulness-based psycho-educational intervention improves depression and clinical symptoms in patients with chronic heart failure. *American Heart Journal, 157*(1): 84–90.

Thompson, R. W., Kaufman, K. A., De Petrillo, L. A., Glass, C. R., & Arnkoff, D. B. (2011). One year follow-up of mindful sport performance enhancement (MSPE) with archers, golfers, and runners. *Journal of Clinical Sport Psychology, 5*(2), 99–116.

Van Aalderen, J. R., Donders, A. R. T., Giommi, F., Spinhoven, P., Barendregt, H. P., & Speckens, A. E. M. (2012). The efficacy of mindfulness-based cognitive therapy in recurrent depressed patients with and without a current depressive episode: A randomized controlled trial. *Psychological Medicine, 42*(05), 989–1001.

Van der Oord, S., Bögels, S. M., & Peijnenburg, D. (2012). The effectiveness of mindfulness training for children with ADHD and mindful parenting for their parents. *Journal of Child and Family Studies, 21*(1), 139–147.

Vitasari, P., Wahab, M., Othman, A., Herawan, T., & Sinnadurai, S. (2010). The relationship between study anxiety and academic performance among engineering students. *ProcediaSocial and Behavioral Sciences, 8,* 490–497.

Vowles, K. E., & McCracken, L. M. (2008). Acceptance and values-based action in chronic pain: A study of treatment effectiveness and process. *Journal of Consulting and Clinical Psychology, 76*(3), 397–407.

Weinberg, R. S. & Gould, D. (2010). *Foundations of sport and exercise psychology*. Champaign, IL: Human Kinetics.

Wenzlaff, R. M., & Wegner, D. M. (2000). Thought suppression. *Annual Review of Psychology, 51*, 59–91.

Willard, C. (2016). *Growing up mindful: Essential practices to help children, teens, and families find balance, calm, and resilience*. Boulder, CO: Sounds True.

Wolanin, A. T. (2005). *Mindfulness-Acceptance-Commitment (MAC) based performance enhancement for Division I collegiate athletes; A preliminary investigation* (Doctoral dissertation, La Salle University, 2003). *Dissertation Abstracts International: Section B, 65*(7), 3735–3794.

Wong, S.Y.S., Yip, B.H.K., Mak, W.W.S., Mercer, S., Cheung, E.Y.L., Ling, C.Y.M., . . . Lee, T.M.C. (2016). Mindfulness-based cognitive therapy v. group psychoeducation for people with generalised anxiety disorder: Randomised controlled trial. *The British Journal of Psychiatry, 209*(1), 68–75.

Zautra, A. J., Davis, M. C., Reich, J. W., Nicassario, P., Tennen, H., Finan, P., . . . Irwin, M. R. (2008). Comparison of cognitive behavioral and mindfulness meditation interventions on adaptation to rheumatoid arthritis for patients with and without history of recurrent depression. *Journal of Consulting and Clinical Psychology, 76*(3): 408.

ORGANIZATIONS

American Mindfulness Research Association: https://goamra.org

The American Mindfulness Research Association's mission is to support empirical and conceptual efforts to establish an evidence base for the process, practice, and construct of mindfulness; promote best evidence-based standards for the use of mindfulness research and its applications; and facilitate discovery and professional development through grant giving.

Center for Mindful Eating: https://www.thecenterformindfuleating.org

The Center for Mindful Eating is a U.S.-based nonprofit and is focused on talking about connecting and teaching professionals and individuals to explore and learn how to apply mindfulness practices to their relationships with food and eating.

Center for Mindfulness: http://www.umassmed.edu/cfm/stress-reduction/history-of-mbsr/.

Established at the University of Massachusetts Medical Center, the Center for Mindfulness advances the health and well-being of society through mind-body research and publication.

UCLA Mindful Awareness Research Center: http://marc.ucla.edu

The UCLA Mindful Awareness Research Center's mission is to foster mindful awareness across the life span through education and research to promote well-being and a more compassionate society.

WEBSITES

Academics

Mindful Schools: http://www.mindfulschools.org/
MindUp: https://mindup.org/

Apps

Calm: www.calm.com
Insight Timer: https://insighttimer.com/

Eating

Mindful Eating: http://www.mb-eat.com/

Mind-Body Medicine

The Benson-Henry Institute for Mind Body Medicine at Massachusetts General Hospital: http://www.massgeneral.org/bhi/

Retreat Centers

Blue Cliff Monastery: https://www.bluecliffmonastery.org/
Deer Park Monastery: http://deerparkmonastery.org/
Desert Renewal: http://desertrenewal.org/
Insight Meditation Society: https://www.dharma.org/
Kripalu Center: https://kripalu.org/
Spirit Rock: http://www.spiritrock.org/

Sports

Mindful Sport Performance Enhancement: http://www.keithkaufman-
phd.com/MSPETraining.en.html

Work

A Head for Work: www.aheadforwork.com/

Index

Academics, 83–84
Acceptance and commitment
    therapy (ACT), 76
Aging, 49, 69
Alcohol, 49–50
Alzheimer's disease, 36–37
Amygdala, 37, 39, 68–69
Anxiety, 7, 9, 12, 26, 28, 37, 45, 47,
    62, 66, 70, 72, 73–74
Apps, 96–98
Athletes, 2, 41, 79, 83, 94
Attention, 3–10, 18–21, 27–39,
    40–46, 55
Attention deficit hyperactivity
    disorder (ADHD), 75
Aurelius, Marcus, 54

Bible, 53, 54, 57
Binge eating disorder, 76, 89
Borderline personality disorder, 62, 75
Brain-imaging, 67
Breath, 10, 15, 18, 25–28
Buddha, 10, 18, 36, 40, 49, 64
Buddhism, 18, 27, 34, 36, 48, 49, 54–56
Business, 86–87, 92

Cancer, 22, 76–77, 90
Catholics, 17, 27, 32, 39, 57, 65, 83
Children, 7, 8, 13, 21, 25–26, 44, 56,
    60, 67, 71, 73, 75, 81, 85, 95
Compassion, 37, 47, 55, 64
Cortisol, 12, 46, 81, 90

Depression, 7, 9, 12, 27, 70, 73–79,
    99–101
Diabetes, 78, 89–90
Dopamine, 8, 95
Drugs, 8, 49–52

Eating, 87–90
Ego, 30, 35, 59
Electronic media, 8, 31, 91–94
Emotions, 4–13, 16, 20, 23, 29, 53,
    57, 60, 68, 80–81
Enlightenment, 16–17, 35–36, 52,
    56, 64
Epictetus, 54
Executive function, 68, 83, 91

Fibromyalgia, 77
Fox, George, 64

Functional magnetic resonance
 imaging (fMRI), 68–69

Garden, 38, 39, 40, 45
Generosity, 35
God, 55, 64, 109
Goleman, Daniel, 93

Hallucinogens, 51–52
Heart, 57, 61, 64, 69, 77, 80, 97, 103
Hinduism, 27, 57–59
HIV, 79
Hunger, 32, 88, 102, 103, 108

Illness, 45, 49, 62, 78, 89
Immune system, 9, 79, 68
India, 39, 49, 59, 61
Intention, 4, 5, 21, 26, 28, 40, 53, 55,
 59, 60, 82, 96
Irritable bowel syndrome, 79
Islam, 27, 59, 64

Jesus Christ, 57, 63, 64
Jewish, 17, 27, 55, 58, 64
Judgment, 6, 18, 21, 26, 29, 33, 44,
 49, 53, 63, 80, 82

Kabat-Zinn, Jon, 3–6, 12, 15, 23,
 61–65, 73, 81, 102
Kabbalah, 58

Lysergic acid diethylamide (LSD),
 51–52

Magnetic resonance spectroscopy, 68
Mantra, 15, 18, 39, 50, 57, 75
Medication, 8, 11, 12, 52, 100–102
Meditator, 10, 19, 23, 27, 40–45,
 56–59, 65, 70, 87
Melatonin, 77
Mindfulness-acceptance-commitment
 (MAC), 82–83
Mindfulness-based cognitive therapy
 (MBCT), 73–74, 81, 100

Mindfulness-based eating awareness
 training (MB-EAT), 89–90, 102
Mindfulness-based relapse prevention
 (MBRP), 73–74
Mindfulness-based stress reduction
 (MBSR), 2–3, 12, 15, 23, 27, 37,
 55, 61, 70–79, 89, 102, 105
Mindfulness-Enhanced
 Strengthening Families Program
 (MSFP), 71
Mindful sport performance
 enhancement (MSPE), 82
Mohammed (prophet), 64
Monastery, 10, 35
Monk, 10, 28, 36, 37, 39, 44, 51, 53,
 57, 61, 66, 96
Music, 38–40, 59, 96, 107

Nature, 46, 108
Neuron, 5, 8, 68
Nhat Hanh, Thich, 97

Obesity, 8, 76, 88, 97, 102

Pain, 27, 28, 33, 37, 45, 59, 62, 70,
 76–78
Paradox, 38, 41, 47, 63
Physical health, 76–81
Positron emission tomography, 68
Post-traumatic stress disorder
 (PTSD), 75
Posture, 14, 15, 30, 45, 90
Prefrontal cortex, 13, 69, 81, 91
Prescription drugs, 52

Quakerism, 64
Quran, 64

Relationships, 8–10, 23, 38, 42,
 47–49, 70–71, 94, 106–8
Relaxation, 9, 10, 14, 37, 40, 62, 81,
 106
Religion, 9, 27, 48, 53–65
Retreat, 31–35, 44, 56, 61–62

Rheumatoid arthritis, 78
Rumi, 59
Rumination, 43, 72, 74, 81

School, 5, 8, 13, 20, 21, 25, 26, 30,
    83–85
Sleep, 9, 11, 29, 102–7
Social media, 7, 21, 88, 94–96, 108
Sports, 22, 54, 79–83

Teacher, 33–35
Tennis, 79–81
Therapist, 42, 72, 100
Therapy, 62, 70, 72, 73–78

Thinking, 5, 6, 17, 21, 39, 41, 57, 68,
    80, 93
Treatment as usual (TAU), 74, 75, 77

Veterans, 75
Vipassana, 31, 42, 67
Vulnerability, 45, 70

Waitlist, 70, 78, 79
Weight, 12, 33, 46, 88, 103–5

Yoga, 10, 14–16, 32–35, 60, 73

Zen, 19, 28, 34–36, 61–62, 109

About the Author

Blaise Aguirre, MD, is an expert in child, adolescent, and adult psychotherapy, including dialectical behavior therapy (DBT) and medication evaluation and management. He is the founding medical director of 3East Girls Intensive and Step-Down Programs, unique, residential DBT programs for young women exhibiting self-endangering behaviors and borderline personality disorder (BPD) traits. Dr. Aguirre has been a staff psychiatrist at McLean Hospital since 2000 and is nationally and internationally recognized for his extensive work in the treatment of mood and personality disorders in adolescents. He lectures regularly in Europe, Africa, and the Middle East on BPD and DBT.

Dr. Aguirre is the author of *Borderline Personality Disorder in Adolescents: A Complete Guide to Understanding and Coping When Your Adolescent Has BPD* and *Depression*. He is a coauthor of *Mindfulness for Borderline Personality Disorder: Relieve Your Suffering Using the Core Skill of Dialectical Behavior Therapy* and *Helping Your Troubled Teen: Learn to Recognize, Understand, and Address the Destructive Behavior of Today's Teens*.